F & SF Ministry For JESUS

What Was Cain's Mark?

Genesis Ch. 4, V. 15

"…And the LORD set a mark upon Cain, lest any finding him should kill him."

Genesis Ch. 4, V. 15

"And the LORD said unto him, Therefore whosoever slayeth Cain, vengeance shall be taken on him sevenfold."

APOSTLE Frederick E. Franklin

authorHOUSE®

AuthorHouse™
1663 Liberty Drive
Bloomington, IN 47403
www.authorhouse.com
Phone: 1-800-839-8640

Published by AuthorHouse 10/20/2014

ISBN: 978-1-4918-2952-3 (sc)
ISBN: 978-1-4918-2951-6 (e)

Library of Congress Control Number: 2013919062

Scripture quotations marked KJV are from the Holy Bible, King
James Version (Authorized Version). First published in 1611. Quoted
from the KJV Classic Reference Bible, Copyright © 1983 by The
HYPERLINK "http://www.zondervan.com/" Zondervan Corporation.

THIS IS A RESUBMISSION/REVISION OF OUR BOOK "WHAT WAS CAIN'S MARK?".

THIS RESUBMISSION/REVISION WAS DONE TO:

1. CORRECT TYPOGRAPHICAL ERRORS;

2. PROVIDE INFORMATION GOD GAVE TO APOSTLE FREDERICK E. FRANKLIN FOR THE BOOK.

These corrections and omissions/additions are necessary due to Apostle Frederick E. Franklin's negligence. In his rush to get (4) four Books published at one time, he did not properly scrutinize the Books for perfection. Also, in his rush to go to New York City to pitch the "The Final Exodus" for a movie to be made of the Book, he was negligent. I HAVE ASKED GOD TO FORGIVE ME. I further ask you to forgive me also.

The four Books referred to above were/are:

1. "WHAT WAS CAIN'S MARK?"

2. "THE FINAL EXODUS"

3. "NEW YORK CITY BECOMES THE CAPITAL OF THE NEW WORLD ORDER"

4. "WHAT GOD IS NOW TELLING HIS PROPHETS ABOUT THE END TIMES".

TABLE OF CONTENTS

INTRODUCTION

This is the (46th) forty-sixth Book which we have written. The scope of this Book has worldwide implications on a natural and spiritual level. The scope of this Book in its importance to the inhabitants of Planet Earth far exceeds our previous Books.

This is a very controversial Book; so controversial to the heights that we needed a special word from God to write it. Once God told us what Cain's Mark was, we knew that this Book would be controversial like never a Book was before. After we were sure that God wanted us to write it, we wrote it. Even after we finished writing the Book, we needed that visitation to release it for publication; even though God was giving us what to write in the Book. It was so controversial or we were such cowards that we needed even more.

This Book tells what Cain's Mark was and is. The revealing of this Mark allows us through this Book to break a stronghold of witchcraft off most of the inhabitants of this earth.

Also this Book, makes it clear who are God's chosen people, unlike as has not been known by them. We not only give revelation from

1

God concerning it, but also provide Scriptural backup.

This Book shows where the United States is talked about in the Holy Scriptures/Bible. This Book points out one of the main end time's roles of the United States on this earth.

This Book explains why the (NRA) National Rifle Association stand on guns is as it is. We even provide Bible evidence of the NRA's stand.

We in this Book, provide what God says or do not say concerning slavery. You will know God's mind regarding this matter.

This Book might turn your world upside down. What you might have thought was good could be shown as bad.

We discuss planetary matters in this Book. We discuss planetary travel in this Book. Is it or is it not? You will know.

In this Book, we discuss sodomy/ homosexuality. We let you know God's view on the matter. This Book tells who are the most hated by God on this earth and it is not the homosexuals/sodomites. This Book let us know why babies and young children are sodomites/homosexuals.

This Book discusses having pets and what God's view of pets are. We show the relationship of your pets to end time's prophecy.

This Book discusses pornography and how it is taken to its repugnant low. We provide testimony concerning pornography. We show its Biblical routes.

We address people talking to a dead love one in this Book. We let you know whether it is true or not. We provide Scriptures to verify what we say.

Yes, this Book again as we have revealed before, tells who the (Anti-Christ) Beast will be. God told us. We, also, in this Book again as we have revealed before, tells who the other Beast, False Prophet, is. God told us.

Yes, all of the above has to do with Cain's mark. Yes, all of it.

Much, much, more we provide in this Book. This Book provides revelation from God directly to us. Also, much, much, more from the Holy Scriptures/Bible of the Old and New Testament we provide.

WHAT WAS CAIN'S MARK ?

This was our (46th) forty-sixth Book which we had written. Before we began to write this Book, we had much prayer to God concerning the writing of it. We believed that God had told us to write it several times, in a span of over a years' time, but we were not sure. We had not received the confirmation from God to write that we were looking for. We had asked God to confirm to us in a vision or dream.

We have written some very controversial books. In fact, most to all of them have had this status. Our books have been so controversial, that when we first tried to get our (1st) first Book published, no one would touch it. We tried different publishers, but no one would touch it. Finally we thought that we had found a publisher, but after having said they would publish it, they later on refused to. After all of our failed attempts to get the Book published, we received, "out of the clear blue", in the next week a letter in the mail from a publisher saying that they would publish our Book no matter how controversial it might be. We knew it had to be God. God had someone to send this promotion to us.

Although our previous books which we accomplished to publish have been controversial, this present Book makes them seem non-controversial in comparison. It is like comparing a mole hill to a mountain. It is like comparing a midget to a professional basketball player who plays center. To satisfy your taste for sweetness, like comparing vinegar to a sun ripened grape.

Due to the extreme level of controversy to what we believed that God was telling us to write, we had to be absolutely sure that it was God telling us to write. We had to be sure, as you will understand as you read this Book.

Finally, on <u>September 23, 2013</u>, we received this confirmation. God told us, indisputably, that we should write this Book.

God let us know that for the publishing of this Book is one of the reasons he had the (1st) First Amendment to be added to the United States' Constitution. The (1st) First Amendment is the Freedom of Speech.

In the beginning of the history of Mankind, after God made Adam and Eve, their first child was born. Their first born was a man child and his name was Cain.

<u>Genesis Ch. 2, V, 7</u>

"And the LORD formed man from the dust of the ground, and breathed into his nostrils the breath of life; and he became a living soul."

You might ask at this point, why did God have to form this man from the dust of the ground, when earlier Scriptures indicated that God created all men and women on the six day? We are ready and very anxious to answer the question concerning forming man from the dust, since the Devil, Satan, has sent out his ministers to lie so grievously concerning this matter. The Devil, Satan, has his ministers saying that Adam and his eventual wife, Eve, were not the first people on this earth. That they were not the beginning of Mankind. Satan uses these lying ministers to pervert the word of God like no others have ever done. There are two of these ministers of Satan that has a worldwide television program. They have deceived and are deceiving all over the world. Satan through these two ministers, also, say that Cain was not Adam's son. They say that Eve committed adultery with Satan. They say that Satan is Cain's father. What stupidity! What ignorance! What perversion! What disregard of God's word! What lies!

Before we go any further, let us clear up this lie since we are talking about man's creation. This is straying away from the main subject, but let us address this matter first.

Genesis Ch. 1, Vs. 26-28

"And God said, Let us make man in our image, after our likeness: and let them have dominion over the fish of the sea, and over the fowl of the air, and over the cattle, and over every creeping thing that creepeth upon the earth. So God created man in his own image, in the image of God created he him; male and female created he them. And God blessed them, and God said unto them, Be fruitful and multiply, and replenish the earth, and subdue it ..."

First of all let us point this out. In the above Scripture, God said, "Be fruitful and multiply, and replenish the earth..." When God created male and female, he created all of the human creation that would ever be. They were spirit beings in heaven and not on this earth. They were in heaven awaiting their appointed time to be born and put on this earth; like any who have not been conceived. Those that are put on earth were to be fruitful, multiply and replenish the earth. "Replenish" means replacing those who die. The spiritual beings created on the six day cannot die. Spirits do not die. Now let us go further.

Unlike what most, nearly all, of the "trinity" believers assert, the Father was not talking to the Son and to the Holy Ghost/Spirit when God said in the above Scriptures "Let us make man in our image and after our likeness". The Father was talking to the angels. When in the beginning God created the heaven and the earth, the angels were created then. Angels did not have to grow up. They were made from the very beginning what they would be. God, himself, told me that he was talking to the angels. Now let us get back on track. Let us get back to the main subject.

God indeed created mankind on the six day; these were spiritual beings created of mankind. This spiritual creation was done in heaven by God; they were and are held in heaven until their appointed time to be born in the flesh. They were and are not on earth until that time. Adam and Eve were the first to receive their earthly bodies. What you must understand, that all things that are natural was first spiritual. God first spoke them to be in the spirit realm and they that were to be earthly, was manifested in the natural. This is further illustrated in Genesis Chapter 2, Verse 19. God had already created creeping things, but here in Genesis Chapter 2, Verse19, it says that God formed them from the ground.

<u>Genesis Ch. 1, Vs. 24 & 25</u>

"And the evening and the morning were the fifth day. And God said, Let the earth bring forth the living creature after his kind, cattle, and creeping thing, and beast of the earth after his kind: and it was so. And God made the beast of the earth after his kind, and cattle after his kind, and every creeping thing that creepeth the earth after his kind: and saw that it was good."

Now far after this time, look at what the Scripture says.

<u>Genesis Ch. 2, V.19</u>

"And out of the ground the LORD formed every beast of the field, and every fowl of the air; and brought them to Adam…"

When man that will be saved die, his soul returns to God. If you are not saved your soul goes to hell.

<u>Ecclessiastes Ch. 12, V. 7</u>

"Then shall the dust return to the earth as it was: and the spirit shall return unto God who gave it."

Remember, understand, your soul is spirit.

Before JESUS' death, burial and resurrection, those that died went into a place that was in the center of the earth. If you were saved, you went to a place called paradise. If you were not saved, lost, the place where you went was across from paradise called hell. Hell is yet where those who die go who are not saved. For those who are saved since JESUS' resurrection, they go into heaven where God is and where the souls/ spirits that have not been born are. As the Scriptures indicate, upon JESUS' resurrection, the souls that were in paradise in the center of the earth came out from there.

<u>Matthew Ch. 27, Vs. 50-53</u>

"Jesus, when he had cried again with a loud voice, yield up the ghost. And behold, the vail of the temple was rent in twain from the top to the bottom; and the earth did quake, and the rocks rent; And the graves were opened; and many bodies of saints which slept arose, after his resurrection, and went into the city, and appeared unto many."

<u>Luke Ch. 16, Vs. 19-26</u>

"There was a certain rich man…And there was a certain beggar named Lazarus…And it came to pass that the beggar died, and was carried by the angels into Abraham's bosom: the rich man also died, and was buried: And in hell he lifted up his eyes, being in torments, and seeth Abraham afar off, and Lazarus in his bosom. And he cried and said, Father Abraham, have mercy on me, and send Lazarus, that he may dip the tip of his finger in water, and cool my tongue; for I am tormented in this flame. But Abraham said, Son, remember that thou in thy lifetime receivedst thy good things, and likewise Lazarus evil things: but now he is comforted, and thou art tormented. And besides all this, between us and you there is a great gulf fixed: so that they which would pass from hence to you cannot;

neither can they pass to us, that would come from thence."

Let us get back to the main subject. Let us get back to the mark of Cain. Let us get back to Adam and Eve. We have shown that God made Adam from the dust of the ground to be the first man upon the earth. God also made Eve to be the first woman. What you must remember that all things that are natural was first spiritual. God spoke them to be in the spirit and they were then manifested in the natural.

Genesis Ch. 2, Vs. 18 & 21-25

"And the LORD said, It is not good that the man should be alone; I will make him a help meet for him. And the LORD caused a deep sleep to fall upon Adam, and he slept: and he took one of his ribs, and closed up the flesh thereof; And the rib, which the LORD God had taken from the man, made he a woman, and brought her unto the man. And Adam said, This is bone of my bones, and flesh of my flesh: she shall be called Woman, because she was taken out of Man. Therefore shall a man leave his father and mother, and shall cleave to his wife: and they shall be one flesh."

Genesis Ch. 3, V. 30

"And Adam called his wife's name Eve; because she was the mother of all living."

After God had eventually kicked Adam and Eve out of the Garden of Eden because Eve was deceived by

Satan and Adam disobeyed God, they, Adam and Eve, eventually had a son called Cain.

<u>Genesis Ch. 4, V. 1</u>

"And Adam knew Eve his wife; and she conceived and bare Cain, and said, I have gotten a man from the LORD."

If Cain had been the son of Satan, as the lying ministers of Satan say, then Eve would not have said, "I have gotten a man from the LORD". To believe otherwise, you must believe that the Scriptures of the Holy Bible is a lie.

These lying ministers of Satan that we mentioned earlier, perverts the word of God in even other ways also. Truly outrageous lies. They even say that you do not burn if you go to hell. They say that the loving God would not allow it to be so; no matter what the Scriptures say. These lying ministers are not saved; they are not born of God. If you are not born of God, born again, you go to hell. No wonder they want to believe that you do not burn when you go to hell. These lying ministers rely on some books of men interpretation of the Holy Scriptures as if the interpreters were God. They claim that in some Greek or Arab or some other language, it says such and such of the Scriptures. Who will you believe, the Holy Scriptures of the Holy Bible or them. They cannot even understand Scriptures written in English, their native tongue, but they want you to believe that they are so intelligent to understand the Scriptures in

11

a language that is not their own. God has warned of these perverters in his word through Apostle Paul.

II Timothy Ch. 3, Vs. 5 & 7

"Having a form of godliness, but denying the power thereof: from such turn away. Ever learning and never able to come to the knowledge of the truth."

After Adam and Eve gave birth to Cain, they also gave birth to a second Son called Abel.

Genesis Ch. 4, V. 2

"And she again bare his brother Abel. And Abel was a keeper of sheep, but Cain was a tiller of the ground."

The Holy Scriptures tell us that Cain would eventually kill his brother Abel because of envy and jealousy. These are the two sins that Lucifer, later to be called Satan, had that caused him to lose his place, power and authority in heaven.

Genesis Ch. 4, Vs. 3-12

"And in the process of time it came to pass, that Cain brought of the fruit of the ground an offering unto the LORD. And Abel, he also brought of the firstlings of his flock and of the fat thereof. And the LORD had respect unto Abel and to his offering: But unto Cain and to his offering he had not respect. And Cain was very wroth, and his countenance fell. And the LORD said unto Cain, Why art thou wroth? And why is thy countenance fallen? If thou doest well, shall thou not be accepted? And if thou doest not well, sin lieth at the door. And unto thee shall be his desire, and thou shall rule over him. And Cain talked with Abel his brother: and it came to pass, when they were in the field, that Cain rose up against Abel his brother, and slew him."

This was, of course, the first murder upon the earth of countless multitudes to come. So here in the above Scriptures we can see a distinguishing trait of the off spring of Cain. They would be murderers and because of their envy and jealousy, they will strive to rule over other human beings. We have written about this in our previous books. God told us that racism is the sin of envy and jealousy. Refer to our Books:

1. "Words From God, By God Appearing To Us Or Just Talking To Us, For The End Times"

2. "God Said Black People In The United States Are Jews"

God also shows us in the Scriptures other distinguishing traits of Cain's off spring.

Genesis Ch. 4, Vs. 9-12

"And the LORD said unto Cain, Where is Abel thy brother? And he said, I know not: Am I my brother's keeper? And he said, What has thou done? The voice of thy brother's blood crieth unto me from the ground. And now art thou cursed from the earth, which hath opened her mouth to received thy brother's blood from thy hand. When thou tillest the ground, it shall not henceforth yield unto thee her strength. A fugitive and vagabond shalt thou be in the earth."

The above Scriptures indicate that the off spring of Cain would readily tell a lie; lying even to and before God himself. Also, the above Scriptures indicate that the off spring of Cain would be lawless, even a fugitive and vagabond. A vagabond is a person that has no permanent land given by God. The person or people would go from place to place, location to location, across the earth. They would not be as China, India or some others. They would try to take over the earth, such as, Alexander The Great, the Roman Empire, the British Empire, Adolph Hitler and the United States. This is what the Scripture of Revelation Chapter 6, Verse 2, is referring to, says God.

Revelation Ch. 6, V. 2

"And I saw, and behold a white horse: and he that sat on him had a bow; a crown was given to him: and he went forth conquering, and to conquer."

Unlike what Satan's ministers say, the above Scripture is not talking about the so-called Anti-Christ, the Beast. Refer to our Books:

1. "The Name Of The (Anti-Christ) Beast And 666 Identification"

2. "What God Is Now Telling His Prophets About The End Times"

The earlier given Scriptures of Genesis Chapter 4, Verses 9-12, also, indicate that the off spring of Cain will not have any land of their own by inheritance and any that they have will be stolen or taken from others.

Another important trait or characteristic of Cain's off spring is the indicated relationship that they would have with God.

Genesis Ch. 4, Vs. 14 & 16

"Behold, thou had driven me out this day from the face of the earth; and from thy face shall I be hid... And Cain went out from the presence of the LORD..."

The above Scriptures indicate that Cain and his off spring would be in idolatry. If God is not man's God, then Satan would be his god. Man is a religious being. Man either worships God or Satan.

John Ch. 8, Vs. 42-44

"Jesus said unto them, If God were your Father, ye would love me: for I proceeded forth and come from God; neither came I of myself, but he sent me. Why do ye not understand my speech? even because ye cannot hear my words. Ye are of your father the devil, and the lusts of your father ye will do. He was a murderer from the beginning, and abode not in the truth, because there is no truth in him. When he speaketh a lie, he speaketh of his own: for he is a liar, and the father of it."

The above statements and Scriptures are why God said what he said to my wife, Prophetess Sylvia Franklin. We will tell you later what God said. It is shocking. Based on all we have read, heard and seen in the different media outlets, it would seem impossible.

There are yet other traits that the Scriptures reveal to us about the offspring's of Cain.

<u>Genesis Ch. 4, Vs. 13-15</u>

"And Cain said unto the LORD, My punishment is more than I can bear, Behold, thou hast driven me out this day from the face of the earth; and from thy face shall I be hid; and I shall be a fugitive and vagabond in the earth; and it shall come to pass, that every one that findeth me shall slay me. And the LORD said unto him, Therefore whosoever slayeth Cain, vengeance shall be taken on him sevenfold. And the LORD set a mark upon Cain, lest any finding him should kill him."

This "mark upon Cain" would have to be something that was easily to be recognized by others. If the vengeance of God would come upon you sevenfold for killing Cain, then the mark would have to be readily and easily seen.

The anthropologists have said that the first man was found in Africa. An anthropologist is one who through science studies the origin of man who does not believe the Holy Scriptures/Bible. The anthropologist's scientific conclusion seems to make sense. There is no mixture of people that will produce a Black man who has been with another ethnic. There is no mixture that will get the hair. There is no mixture that will get the facial features. So then, Adam and Eve were Black.

The mark would have to be indisputable. It would have to be something that would make Cain stand out from everyone else. Cain could not look like Adam. Cain could not look like Eve. Cain could not look like Adam's and Eve's third son Seth. There had to be something about Cain that was different from these three Black people. God revealed to us that this difference was that Cain's curse by him was with a curse in his pigmentation of his skin. His skin was bleached of its color. His skin was made pale. Even his hair was bleached; Cain was the first blond. So says God. So, Cain looked like what we call white people, Caucasians. Cain was the first Caucasians. This way everyone could easily and readily recognize Cain. This curse by God left Cain's face and skin pale; unlike the Black Adam, Eve and Seth. SO SAYS GOD!

There are further traits or characteristics about Cain's off spring that the Scriptures reveal. You might wonder, where did Cain get a wife from? Cain's wife was a daughter of Adam and Eve. So says God.

Genesis Ch. 4, Vs. 17-19 & 22

"And Cain knew his wife, and she conceived, and bare Enoch: and he build a city, after the name of his son, Enoch. And unto Enoch was born Irad: and Irad begat Mehujael, and Mehujael begat Methusael: and Methusael begat Lamech. And Lamech took upon him two wives: the name of one was Adah, and the name of the other Zillah. And Zillah, she also bare Tubal-cain, an instructor of every artificer in brass and iron…"

The above Scriptures indicate that the off spring of Cain would master the use of brass and iron. Brass and iron were the beginning of the weapons to kill other people. The Scriptures above also pins down a name that can be traced to other places in the Holy Scriptures/Bible, "Tubal-cain".

Noah's son Japhet married the daughter of Cain's off spring. Japhet's line can be traced to the Europeans. Also, we see Tubal of "Tubal-cain" mentioned in the Holy Scriptures in the Book of Ezekiel.

Genesis Ch. 10, V. 2

"The sons of Japheth; Gomer, and Magog, and Madia, and Javan, and Tubal, and Meshech, and Tiras."

Ezekiel Ch. 38, Vs. 2 & 3

"Son of man, set thy face against Gog, the land of Magog, the chief prince of Meshech and Tubal, and prophesy against him, And say, Thus saith the LORD GOD; Behold, I am against thee, O Gog, the chief prince of Meshech and Tubal…"

Magog is called in these days/times Russia. Gog is the leader of Russia.

We see that Tubal and other off spring of Cain were slave owners. Where have we heard of this before?

Ezekiel Ch. 27, V.13

"Javan, Tubal, Meshech, they were thy merchants: they traded the persons of men and vessels of brass in thy market."

There has not been since the days of Egypt of old that a people were known for slave trading, except for the Europeans. These certain people were called the enemies of God's people.

Genesis Ch. 22, V. 17

"That in blessing I will bless thee, and in multiplying I will multiply thy seed as the stars of the heaven, and as the sand which is upon the sea shore; and thy seed shall possess the gate of his enemies…"

Deuteronomy Ch. 28, V.68

"And the LORD shall bring thee into Egypt again with ships, by the way whereof I spake and there ye shall be sold unto your enemies for bondmen and bondwomen, and no man shall buy you."

Egypt in the above Scripture is referring to the United States. The United States in the Holy Scriptures of the Holy Bible is referred to as:

1. Egypt

2. Sodom

3. The Great City

4. Babylon The Great/The Great Babylon/ Babylon

5. Harlot

6. Whore

7. Mystery

8. The Mother Of Harlots

9. Abominations Of The Earth

10. Woman

As we have written in other of our books, God himself told me that the United States is Babylon The Great. I will again testify of this revelation. God gave me a dream. In the dream, God and I were side by side. God was on the left of me. We were up high looking down on the earth. I do not know whether we were in the first heaven, second heaven or third heaven. All of a sudden God opened up a very large and very thick Book to me. This I understood somehow, through revelation to my mine, as God told me, was the Book that contained every event of the history of mankind. God then opened the Book to the back part of the back of the Book. As God then turned the pages toward the end of the Book, the written words on the page of the Book became a vision. We were looking down on the vision. God let me know that He was showing me the future. The vision was about the size of a football field; about (100) one hundred yards long and (50) fifty hundred yards wide. I will not tell you everything that God showed me. I will, however, tell you what God told me and showed me as it relates to showing that the United States is Babylon The Great. As God turned the page of future events, I saw missiles flying through the air. These missiles were arrayed in pattern like as fowl flying through the sky in winter migration. These missiles, God let me know that they were of the nuclear and poison gas variety. As God then again turned the page, the written words again became a large vision that we were looking down on. In this vision of the future God showed me fire and explosion happening somewhere on earth. Again as God turned the page and the corresponding vision appeared, there in the vision were large fowl somewhere on the earth. These fowl were nasty. They were vomiting. They were filthy. They looked retarded and deformed. God told me to open up my Bible of the Holy Scriptures and turn to Revelation Chapter 18 and read.

<u>Revelation Ch. 18, Vs. 1 & 2</u>

"And after these things I saw another angel come down from heaven, having great power; and the earth was lightened with his glory. And he cried mightily with a strong voice, saying, Babylon the great is fallen, is fallen, and is become the habitation of devils, and the hold of every fowl spirit, and a cage of every unclean and hateful bird."

God told me after reading the above Scriptures, that the "cage of every unclean and hateful" were those nasty, filthy, vomiting and retarded and deformed fowl that I saw in the vision. God, also, said that these fowl were in the condition they were in because of the missiles that I saw in the vision. God said that these fowl were like this because they were contaminated by the nuclear and poison gas bombing. This bombing, God told me, was the fire and explosions that I saw in the vision. God told me that this fire and explosion was happening in the United States and that the United States is Babylon the Great.

God also showed me in the visions during this time, how many would be saved in the United States. As God turned the page, a still vision appeared. This still vision was also about the length of a football field. The still vision was merely a number. It was the number of souls that will be saved in the United States. I thought that my eyes were deceiving me. I was shocked. It was amazing. I was astounded. I saw the exact number of those who would be saved in the United States. I saw the exact number that would be in the First Resurrection, the so-called rapture. The number was not (148,000,000) one hundred forty eight million. The number was not (14,800,000) fourteen million eight hundred thousand. The number was not (1,480,000) million four hundred eighty thousand. The number, shockingly, was (148,000) one hundred forty eight thousand. Yes, only (148,000) one hundred forty eight thousand souls will be saved in the United States. The United States, the so-called Christian nation; a nation of over (300,000,000) three hundred million. Refer to our Books:

1. "United States In The Bible"

2. "The Judgment Of The United States"

3. "Words From God, By God Appearing To Us Or Just Talking To Us, For The End Times"

4. "The Ten Horns Of The Books Of Daniel And Revelation"

Remember this regarding Deuteronomy Chapter 28, Verse 68, in Egypt of old, the slaves, God's people, the children of Israel, did not go there by way of ships.

Deuteronomy Ch. 28, V. 68

"And the LORD shall bring thee into Egypt again with ships, by the way whereof I spake and ye shall be sold unto your enemies for bondmen and bondwomen..."

Revelation Ch. 17, Vs. 4 & 5

"And the woman was arrayed in purple and scarlet colour, and decked with gold and precious stones and pearls, having a golden cup in her hand full of abominations and filthiness of her fornication: And upon her head was a name written, MYSTERY, BABYLON THE GREAT, THE MOTHER OF HARLOTS AND ABOMINATIONS OF THE EARTH."

Revelation Ch. 17, V. 18

"And the woman which thou sawest is that great city, which reigneth over the kings of the earth."

Revelation Ch. 18, Vs. 8-10

"Therefore shall her plagues come in one day, death, and mourning, and famine; and she shall be utterly burnt with fire: for strong is the LORD God who judgeth her. And the kings of the earth, who have committed fornication and lived deliciously with her, shall bewail her, and lament for her, when they shall see the smoke of her burning. Standing afar off for the fear of her torment, saying, Alas, alas, that great city Babylon, that mighty city! For in one hour is thy judgment come."

In the above Scriptures, they were standing far off for fear of contamination of the nuclear and poison gas bombing.

Revelation Ch. 18, Vs. 16-18

"…Alas, alas, that great city…For in one hour so great riches has come to nought. And every shipmaster, and all the company in ships, and sailers, and as many as trade by sea, stood afar off, And cried when they saw the smoke of her burning, saying, What city is like unto this great city?"

Revelation Ch. 18, V. 21

"And a mighty angel took up a great millstone, and cast it unto the sea, saying, Thus with violence shall that great city Babylon be thrown down, and shall not be found no more at all."

Revelation Ch. 11, Vs. 3,7 & 8

"And I will give power unto my two witnesses…And when they shall have finished their testimony, the beast… shall…kill them. And their dead bodies shall lie in the <u>street of the great city,</u> which spiritually is called Sodom and Egypt, where also our Lord was crucified."

Many and most have thought, incorrectly, that the two witnesses will be killed in Jerusalem because of the part of the above Scripture which say "where also our Lord was crucified". The correct interpretation is that the two witnesses' "dead bodies shall lie in the street", just as the Lord was crucified in the street. So, therefore, the Great City is also called Sodom; which is also called Egypt; which is also called Babylon The Great; which is the United States of America.

Deuteronomy Ch. 28, V. 68

"And the Lord shall bring thee into Egypt again with ships, by the way thereof I spake unto thee, thou shall see it no more again: and there ye shall be sold unto your enemies for bondmen and bond women, and no man shall buy you."

So, we see that God told us before, even during Moses' day, that Tubal and others of the off spring of Cain, would have slaves of God's people in the United States.

Ezekiel Ch. 27, V. 13

"Javan, Tubal, and Meshech, they were thy merchants: they traded the persons of men, and vessels of brass and iron in thy markets."

Another indication that Babylon the Great is the United States can be seen in the Scriptures reference to Babylon the Great as having slaves in the latter days.

<u>Revelation Ch. 18, Vs. 10-13</u>

"...that great city Babylon...the merchants of the earth shall weep and mourn over her; for no man buyeth their merchandise any more: The merchandise of... slaves..."

Some of Cain's off spring, white folks, pale people, have said that God is not against slavery to justify their slavery efforts across the earth. They have said that God meant it to be so that Black People are to be slaves. They have also said that God did not say anything against slavery in his word. All of the above in this paragraph is not true concerning God. Not only is it shown not to be true through God bringing judgment against the perpetrators of slavery, but also God even says in his word that the benefits that might be gain from slavery is an abomination to him.

<u>Deuteronomy Ch. 23, V. 18</u>

"Thou shall not bring the hire of a whore, or the price of a dog into the house of the LORD thy God for any vow: for even both these are abomination unto the LORD thy God."

The "price of a dog" in the above Scripture is referring to a person being sold as a slave; even a gentile being sold as a slave. This means that any of the riches incurred by white people having slaves is an abomination to God. God does not want your tithes and offerings resulting from your benefit of slavery. If your tithes and offerings are abominations to God, so are you an abomination to God. No wonder why so very few white people will be saved, will be in the first resurrection, the so-called rapture. So says God. Here is the seemingly impossible based on the media propaganda that we said we would tell you. God told my wife, Prophetess Sylvia Franklin, in around the Year of 2009, that there were NO WHITE PEOPLE SAVED IN BIBLICAL TIMES.

Another reference to God being against slavery is also shown in the Book of Proverbs of the Holy Scriptures/ Bible. The Book of Proverbs was written by the wises man who had ever lived at that time. Not only that, Proverbs were given by the creator of wisdom, the Almighty God, the Creator of all things.

Proverbs Ch. 16, V. 26

"He that laboureth laboureth for himself; for his mouth craveth it of him."

Here in the above Scripture God says that a man's work is to benefit him. A man's labor is primarily for his own benefit and not to benefit another, such as, a slave master. God, therefore, denounces slavery.

The lying ministers of Satan mentioned earlier and some other lying ministers of Satan, say that the children of Israel were and are the white people, Caucasians. This can very easily be shown to be a lie. Not only is this shown to be a lie of what God told my wife, Prophetess Sylvia Franklin, when God said that no white people were saved during Biblical times, but it also can be shown to be a lie in other ways.

When the children of Israel came out of Egypt it was about (3,000,000) three million of them. If we consider the death of the children of Israel due to the judgment of God in the wilderness before they came to the promise land, that number was significant, but not relative to the total number of the children of Israel. So consider that number, plus God said that no man over the age of twenty would enter into the promise land; until they all died of natural death or the judgment of God. So, therefore, the natural state of things were happening. People were dying and people being born.

Understand/Remember, that when the children of Israel went out from Egypt, there was not one feeble among them.

Exodus Ch. 15, V. 26

"…for I am the LORD that healeth thee."

Deuteronomy Ch. 29, V. 5

"And I have led you forty years in the wilderness: your clothes are not waxen old upon you and thy shoe is not waxen old upon thy foot."

Deuteronomy Ch. 34, V. 7

"And Moses was an hundred and twenty years old when he died: his eye was not dim, nor his natural force abated."

Psalm 105, Vs. 36-37

"He smote also all the firstborn in their land, the chief of all their strength. He brought them forth also with silver and gold: and there was not one feeble person among their tribes."

The children of Israel were in good health when they went out of Egypt; all of them. This also indicate that they were all in good health in the (40) forty years in the wilderness; except for God's judgment of the snake bites.

For simplification of calculation, using very conservative figures, let us just assume that when the children of Israel went into the promise land after (40) forty years, that the number of them were yet only (3,000,000) three million. If we assume that out of the (3,000,000) three million of the children of Israel, half were females. After about (20) twenty years, all of these women would be of child bearing age. Understand this, the children of Israel had large families. Out of (3,000,000) of the children of Israel, we can assume that half of them were females which equals 1,500,000 females. Let us assume a conservative 5 children for each family; assume after about 20 years all the females leaving out of Egypt would be of child bearing age; assume only half were not too old to have children which would be 750,000 women; then

750,000 x 5 + 3,000,000 =

3,750,000 + 3,000,000 = <u>6,750,000 children of Israel after just 20 years.</u>

Assume half are women of the 6,750,000, then there would be 3,375,000 women. Assume only half bore children which would be 1,687,500 women; then

1,687,500 x 5 + 6,750,000 =

8,437,500 + 6,750,000 = <u>15,187,500 children of Israel after 40 years.</u>

Now assume that only half of the adult population will be living after 20 years;

Assume half are women of the 15,187,500, then there would be about 7,500,000 women; assume half of that number bore children; then there would be 3,750,000 child bearing women; half of the adult population being dead after 20 years would leave 7,500,000; then

3,750,000 x 5 + 7,500,000 =

18,750,000 + 7,500,000 = <u>26,250,000 children after just 60 years.</u>

Assume half are women of the 26,250,000, then there would be about 13,125,000 women. Assume half of that number bore children; then there would be 6,562,500 child bearing women; half of the adult population being dead after 20 years would leave 13,125,000; then

6,562,500 x 5 + 13,125,000 =

32,812,500 + 13,125,000 = 45,937,500 <u>children of Israel after just 80 years.</u>

Assume half are women of the 45,937,500, then there would be 22,968,750 females. Assume half of that number bore children; then there would be 11,484,375 child bearing women; half of the adult population being dead after 20 years would leave 22,175,750; then

11,484,375 x 5 + 22,175,750 =

57,421,875 + 22,175,750 = 79,597,625 <u>children of Israel after just 100 years.</u>

Assume half are females of the 79,597,625, then there would be about 39,798,813 females. Assume half of that number bore children; then there would be 19,899,407 child bearing women; half of the adult population being dead after 20 years would leave 39,798,813; then

19,899,407 x 5 + 39,798,813 =

99,497,035 + 39,798,813 = 139,295,848 <u>children of Israel after just 120 years.</u>

Assume half are females of the 139,295,848, then there would be 69,647,924 females. Assume half of that number bore children; then there would be 34,823,962 children bearing women; half of the adult population being dead after 20 years would leave 69,647,924; then

34,823,962 x 5 + 69,647,924 =

174,119,810 + 69,647,924 = 243,767,734 <u>children of Israel after just 140 years.</u>

Assume half are females of the 243,767,734, then there would be 121,883,867 females. Assume half of that number bore children; then there would be 60,941,934 child bearing women; half of the adult population being dead after 20 years would leave 121,883,867; then

60,941,934 x 5 + 121,883,867 =

304,709,670 + 121,883,867 = 426,593,537 <u>children of Israel after just 160 years. After 180 years, the number of the Israelites would equal 746,538,694.</u>

Now this is not an exact number, but it gives you an idea. This, however, let you know that the around (500,000,000) five hundred million, white people that is now on the earth, could not be the children of Israel. After just a (180) one hundred eighty years after the children Israel came out of the wilderness to go into the promise land, there were more of the children of Israel than it is of all white people, pale people, Caucasians, that is now on the earth. Also, God said that with the children of Israel, that he would increase their numbers to a very great amount. Being in the minority as the Caucasians are, does not line up with what God said.

<u>Genesis Ch. 22, V. 17</u>

"That in blessing I will bless thee, and in multiplying I will multiply thy seed as the stars of the heaven, and as the sand which is upon the sea shore…"

Therefore, we have proved that those lying ministers of Satan who say that the white people, Caucasians, pale people, of Europe are the children of Israel is a lie. A flat out lie!

The murdering spirit of Cain's off spring, white people, pale people, is a prevailing life style with this people. They have exported their terror throughout the earth.

Ezekiel Ch. 32, V. 26

"There is Meshech, Tubal, and all her multitude: her graves are round him: all of them uncircumcised, slain by the sword, though they caused their terror in the land of the living."

This murdering by the off spring of Cain, pale people, white people, was establish from the very beginning. Not only was Cain himself the first to commit murder, but the second murder on this earth was committed by Cain's off spring, pale people, white people.

Genesis Ch. 4, Vs. 23 & 24

"And Lamech said unto his wives, Adah and Zillah, hear my voice; ye wives of Lamech, hearken to my speech: for I have slain a man to my wounding, and a young man to my hurt. If Cain shall be avenged sevenfold, truly Lamech seventy and sevenfold."

You might wonder, why did God tell Cain that if anyone would kill him, they would suffer a sevenfold punishment. God himself threatened mankind with a sevenfold judgment.

Genesis Ch. 4, V. 15

"And the LORD said unto him, Therefore whosoever slayeth Cain, vengeance shall be taken on him sevenfold. And the LORD set a mark upon Cain lest any finding him should kill him."

God needed such as Cain in a similar way that JESUS needed Judas Iscariot. If Cain had been killed then the Plan of God for Mankind could not be completed.

John Ch. 6, Vs. 70 &71

"Jesus answered them, Have not I chosen you twelve, and one of you is a devil? He spake of Judas Iscariot the son of Simon: for he it was that should betray him, being one of the twelve."

Isaiah Ch. 45, V. 7

"I formed the light, and create darkness: I make peace, and create evil: I the LORD do all these things."

You can see God using the evil of this world through his use of the (Anti-Christ) Beast. God says that he will use the (Anti-Christ) Beast to do his will.

Revelation Ch. 17, Vs. 16-17

"And the ten horns which thou sawest upon the beast, these shall hate the whore, and shall make her desolate and naked, and shall eat her flesh, and burn her with fire. For God hath put in their hearts to fulfill his will, and to agree, and to give their kingdom unto the beast, until the words of God shall be fulfilled."

God therefore needed such as Cain. Looking down through the history of Mankind, God could see how a murderer would be necessary to carry out his Plan for Mankind. God could see that such a people of the off spring of Cain, pale people, white people, having Cain's attributes would be essential for God's Plan to redeem Mankind.

Right now in the United States the spirit of Cain is dominating the News and Congressional action and discourse. This murdering spirit of Cain has a strong anchor with the (NRA) National Rifle Association. The discourse by the NRA to defend having weapons of mass murder seems unbelievable to those of us who are sane. Only a heathen and barbaric people would defend arming the general population with these murdering machines. The spirit of Cain has truly reached its height in the United States. Making it easy to butcher another human being is what that is being argued. How barbaric is this?

Also, the spirit of Cain is on full display in the United States massive military complex. The United States spending on its military is more than the next (10) ten largest militaries in the world.

Even as we write this Book, April 15, 2013, the murdering spirit of Cain is on dramatic and full display. We are referring to the bombing in the City of Boston, Massachusetts. Boston is a famous city in the United States. It is known worldwide for many things. Boston is known for its historical and political importance in the United States. Boston is also known worldwide for its athletic endeavors, among them are:

1. Boston Celtics Professional Basketball Team;

2. Boston Red Sox Professional Baseball Team;

3. Boston Bruins Professional Hockey Team;

4. Boston Marathon

The Boston Marathon, however, might be what Boston is known for from now on. This is because while we are writing this Book, during the time of the Boston Marathon, there were two bombings. The bombings were about (15) fifteen seconds apart. There were (3) three people killed and about (280) two hundred and eighty people who were wounded. Among the number that were killed and injured were children. This happened at a time when the whole world was watching the Boston Marathon. The Marathon had participants from all over the world.

The slaughter of the citizens was and is not a rarity in the United States. As of April 15, 2013, there have been approaching (4,000) four thousand murders in the United States, for this year. Over (30,000) thirty thousand people are killed every year in the United States. This is more than half of the people that were killed of the United States in the Vietnam War. Bye the way, in that murderous war, that was unprovoked, the United States killed over a million people. I ask you, is the spirit of Cain live and well in the United States? Bye the way, less we forget, the United States as a country, was established by murdering the original inhabitants, the Indians, of this land.

God told me several years ago, that guns have evil
spirits associated with them. The guns were made
to kill another person, therefore, Satan and the evil
spirits have possessed these weapons of murder. You
can actually feel the spirits associated with them.
As soon as you pick up a gun, an evil spirit comes
upon you. God said to me that guns are Satanic and
demonic. That is why it is so easy to kill when you
have a gun in your hand. That is why the (NRA)
National Rifle Association and the gun manufacturers
seem so evil. God said it! I remember when I was a
young man, a teenager, my first cousin and I were
hunting. We were in a thick wooded area in a place/
community called Dawes in Mobile, Alabama here
in the United States. We had got separated while
hunting. I called out for my cousin to see where he
was. Well, I later saw him, but he did not know that I
saw him. He was trying to slip up behind me to scare
me. I could clearly see all he was trying to do. I could
see it all plainly. I knew what he was doing. So, I
pretended to not see him and let him supposedly scare
me. So he came up behind me and said boo to scare
me. I knew exactly that he was going to do this. When
he said boo, I turned around with the gun and almost
pulled the trigger. I stopped just in the instant of time
from killing him. It was like a spirit took over me. I
know now that this was exactly what happened.

What happened in the hunting experience, also
happened another time. When I was young man, in
my twenties, I was living in Cleveland, Ohio of the
United States. I was not married and not saved at that
time. I for some reason had bought a pistol and started

carrying it on me. I was with a certain woman and she said something that I did not like, I pulled out my pistol and was getting ready to pull the trigger, to kill her. I stopped just in the instant of time before I pulled the trigger. It was like my sound mind came back to me before I pulled the trigger. I said to myself, what in the world is this that I was about to do. I know now that it was God who ran those evil spirits from me. Very soon after that experience, I came from Cleveland on a vacation to Mobile, Alabama. This is where I am now writing this Book, where my family and I live. On this vacation, my cousin, that I mentioned earlier, and I were fishing. We were fishing in about the same place where I almost killed him when we hunting. I had the pistol in my holster that I bought in Cleveland with me. We were fishing in a very shallow stream of the creek, about a foot deep. It was clear water. We could see the bottom of the creek. I leaned over to put my hook in the water and the pistol fell out of my holster into the clear water about a foot from me. My cousin and I searched the clear, shallow, water for about an hour looking for the pistol and never found it. I know now that it was God that caused me to lose that pistol/gun. I probably would have killed someone. God just had an angel to hide that pistol so we could not find it. Satan would have made me kill someone.

We know that God has a Plan for Mankind, but Satan also has a Plan for Mankind. Consider what would Satan's Plan be? What would Satan who hates Mankind Plan be? What would Satan who is jealous and envious of Mankind Plan be? Satan who is a murderer, what would his Plan for Mankind be? Well, Satan would base his Plan on efforts to combat God's Plan for Mankind. God's Plan for Mankind is to save Mankind. It is God's desire that we would all be saved.

<u>II Peter Ch. 3, V. 9</u>

"The Lord is not slack concerning his promise, as some men count slackness; but is longsuffering to us-ward, not willing that any should perish, but that all should come to repentance."

Every since Adam and Eve listened to the voice of Satan in the Garden of Eden and, therefore, denounced the God Almighty and were kicked out of the Garden of Eden, God has a had a Plan in the making to redeem Mankind. The Plan was fully executed when JESUS died on the cross and was buried and rose from the dead after three days and three nights. Well, Satan's Plan is that he will simply deceive Mankind not to believe what JESUS has said. Satan's main source of this deception is carried out through his preachers, such as, those two that we mentioned earlier. JESUS said, to be redeemed, to be saved, that you must be born again and then obey God's word. Born again means to be born of God. What do you imagine what Satan would be Planning to combat this. Satan would simply have his ministers to establish a lie on being born of God.

John Ch. 3, Vs. 3 & 5

"Jesus answered and said unto him, Verily, verily, I say unto thee, Except a man be born again, he cannot see the kingdom of God. Jesus answered, Verily, verily, I say unto thee, Except a man be born of water and of the Spirit, he cannot enter into the kingdom of God."

Later in this Book we provide you with four easy steps how to be born again.

Satan has known about God's Plan to redeem Mankind for many years; every since Adam and Eve's time.

Genesis Ch. 3, V. 15

"And I will put enmity between thee and the woman, and between thy seed and her seed; it shall bruise thy head, and thou shalt bruise his heel."

So, Satan has been at work every since the days of Adam and Eve to carry out his Plan for Mankind. What do you think a cunning Planner would do? He would of course try to influence how Mankind thinks. He would understand that since God mentioned that man's off spring would be against him, but some for him, then, therefore, Satan saw his opportunity. Satan saw that God was pleased with Abel and not pleased with Cain. Satan's most characteristic sins and first sins were jealousy and envy. Satan, therefore, imparted these two sins, jealousy and envy, into Cain, thereby, causing Cain to kill Abel. As time passed, Satan saw how easy it was to control Mankind. As history continued to shed time, Satan noticed that God said through Solomon, God's wises servant, that money could control all things.

Ecclesiastes Ch. 10, V. 19

"A feast is made for laughter, and wine maketh merry: but money answered all things."

Understanding this, Satan launched an all-out effort to get money into the hands of those who would be most useful to him. Satan surmised that if he could get money into the hands of the most ignorant and stupid of Mankind, then he would have a great advantage in this war for souls. So Satan has made sure that the most ignorant and stupid would control the riches of the world; which turned out to be Cain's off spring, pale people.

Most of the mental retarded and mentally disturbed among people is nothing more than demon/unclean spirit/evil spirit possession. Most of this possession comes from witchcraft or sodomy/homosexuality. Most of this demon/unclean spirit/evil spirit possession is called:

1. Down Syndrome

2. Autism

3. Schizophrenia

4. Etc.

These have been the names given by the Psychiatrist. Who themselves are nothing more than witchcraft workers. God says that the demon/unclean spirit/ evil spirit should be cast out of people. To do this, you must have the Spirit, the Holy Ghost. If you have God's Spirit you speak in tongues. The world's and Satan's answer to the problem of this possession is to take the counsel of a Psychiatrist. JESUS said that a devil cannot cast out a devil. Thus you have the Psychiatrist's counsel/advice.

Matthew Ch. 12, Vs. 22-28

"Then was brought unto him one possessed with a devil, blind, and dumb: and he healed him, insomuch that the blind and dumb both spake and saw. And all the people were amazed, and said, Is this the son of David? But when the Pharisees heard it, they said, This fellow doth not cast out devils, but by Beelzebub the prince of devils. And Jesus knew their thoughts, and said unto them, Every kingdom divided against itself is brought to desolation; and every city or house divided against itself shall not stand: And if Satan cast out Satan, he is divided against himself; how shall then his kingdom stand? And if Beelzebub cast out devils, by whom do your children cast them out? Therefore they shall be your judges. But I cast out devils by the Spirit of God…"

Most of this mental retardation or mental problems are among Cain's off spring, pale people, white folks. It is not hardly a family among them who do not have this mental retardation or mental problems. This is because it is not hardly a family among them who are not demon/unclean spirit/evil spirit possessed. This is because it is not hardly a family among them who do not practice witchcraft and who are not homosexuals.

Consider this. Suppose that you gathered all of these demon/unclean spirit/evil spirit possessed people together and make a society of them and give them all the money to do what they want. What would you eventually get? You would get Cain's off spring, pale people, white folks. You would get such as the United States, Great Britain, Russia and the other European societies. God, himself, told and showed me back in the summer of the Year of 2000, that Former President George W. Bush was like a mentally retarded child.

You might say, I do not believe that such scheming has been done to control mankind by Satan. I say to you, yes it has been and yes it is. I have not written of this before. Not in all of our previous other (45) forty-five Books, have I written this. God took me to another planet. I was on a mission for God, but I do not know what the mission was. God put me in a large building complex on the planet. I was there spying on the occupants of the building complex. I knew, somehow through God's revelation to my mine, that if they caught me they would kill me. I would be dead. There were men there in the building complex. They were dressed in clothing of modern day suits; such as would be in a typical office job in our society here in the United States. These men, and they all were men, were constantly planning evil. Every imagination, every word and every deed of theirs were evil. As I continued to spy and observe them, I was discovered by them. They were about to catch me and kill me and just at that moment God translated me to heaven. I will not tell any more at this time. These men on this planet were Satan's helpers; fallen angels or demons, evil spirits or whatever you want to call them. They were constantly and continually planning evil. This planning of the evil spirits/fallen angels was against God and Mankind. These helpers of Satan were on another planet. I do not know what planet. Angels, including fallen angels, evil spirits, look like human beings. Remember, God said let us make man in our own image.

Genesis Ch. 1, Vs. 26 & 27

"And God said let us make man in our own image, after our likeness…So God created man in his own image, in the image of God created he him…"

Also, the Book of Hebrews of the New Testament of the Holy Scriptures/Bible indicates that fallen angels/ evil spirits look like men.

Hebrews Ch. 13, V. 2

"Be not forgetful to entertain strangers: for thereby some have entertained angels unawares."

The evil spirit/fallen angel/familiar spirit is who people see when they say that they saw or spoke to a dead person who they recognized that was not saved. Let us be clear here. No one is or has been saved unless he or she spoke in tongues. You might say, I KNOW THAT MY MOTHER, FATHER, CHILD OR WHOEVER WAS SAVED and they did not speak in tongues. If you know that they were saved, then we say unto you, they spoke in tongues before they died at some point and time and you just did not know it. For those who were not saved or who are saved, neither they nor Satan nor any of his helpers, has any power to get anyone out of hell or heaven. They pretend to do so to get your money. Some have pointed to the Holy Scriptures of I Samuel Chapter 28, regarding Saul talking to the witch of Endor, to say that a witch or warlock/wizard can bring someone back from the dead. They, the witch or warlock/wizard, sadly misrepresent the Scriptures to you. You, as well as they, are ignorant of God's word. You must remember/understand at this point and time that God had rejected Saul and turned him over to lying spirits.

<u>I Samuel Ch. 28, Vs. 7-14</u>

"Then said Saul unto his servants, Seek me a woman that hath a familiar spirit, that I may go to her, and inquire of her. And his servant said to him, Behold, there is a woman that hath a familiar spirit at Endor. And Saul disguised himself, and put on other raiment, and he went, and two men with him, and they came to the woman by night: and he said, I pray thee, divine unto me by the familiar spirit, and bring me him up, whom I shall name unto thee. And the woman said unto him, Behold, thou knowest what Saul hath done, how he hath cut off those that have familiar spirits, and the wizards, out of the land: where then layest thou a snare for my life, to caused me to die? And Saul sware to her by the LORD, saying, As the LORD liveth, there shall no punishment happen to thee for this thing. Then said the woman, Whom shall I bring up unto thee? And he said, Bring me up Samuel. And when the woman saw Samuel, she cried with a loud voice: and the woman spake to Saul, saying, Why hath thou deceived me? for thou art Saul. And the king said unto her, Be not afraid: for what sawest thou? And the woman said unto Saul, I saw gods ascending out of the earth. And he said unto her, What form is he of? And she said, An old man cometh up; and he is covered with a mantle. And Saul perceived that it was Samuel, and he stooped with his face to the ground, and bowed himself."

The above Scriptures are what the witches and wizards/warlocks use to trick the people that they are calling up someone from the dead. The "familiar spirit" tag is so-called because the demon/evil spirit/familiar spirit is pretending to be the person supposedly called up from the dead. The spirit is imitating the dead person. These witches and wizards/warlocks know it. THEY TRICK YOU TO GET YOUR MONEY. God had Samuel to appear before the witch could even start practicing her witchcraft. Look again at those Scriptures. It was said, "Then said the woman, Whom shall I bring up unto thee? And he said, bring me up Samuel. And when the woman saw Samuel, she cried with a loud voice." The witch was surprised. Why was she surprised? She was use to the demon/evil spirit/familiar spirit pretending to be the person. The woman was surprised because God had Samuel to appear. God did it. God did it before the witch and the familiar spirit could begin there deceit.

Many people practice witchcraft and do not know it. They do not understand that when they go to those witches, wizards/warlocks, palm readers, psychics, magicians and the likes, they are practicing witchcraft.

It is almost a guarantee, that when you go from God, you go into witchcraft. This includes people who God has withdrawn his Spirit from. So, when Cain went out from the presence of God, he went into witchcraft.

<u>Genesis Ch. 4, V. 16</u>

"And Cain went out from the presence of the LORD, and dwelt in the land of Nod, on the east of Eden."

Let us give you this further counsel concerning something that we said earlier. We mentioned that God translated me to another planet where there were evil spirits there planning evil. There are not any other human beings on other planets. However, this experience of God taking me to another planet where there were evil spirits on it, let me know that there might be other of God's creation, other than human beings, that could be on other planets. For all of you who somehow think that you can go to another planet to escape God's judgment, you are mistaken.

<u>Acts Ch. 17, Vs. 24 & 26</u>

"God...hath made of one blood all nations of men for to dwell on all the face of the earth, and hath determined the times before appointed, and the bounds of their habitation..."

The idea of other human beings living on other planets is a lie from Satan. Satan perverts God's word in the Holy Scriptures of Ezekiel Chapter 1 of the Old Testament.

<u>Ezekiel Ch. 1, Vs. 4-28 & Ch. 3, Vs. 12-14</u>

"And I looked, and behold, a whirlwind came out of the north, a great cloud, and a fire infolding itself, and a brightness was about it, and out of the midst thereof as the colour of amber, out of the midst of the fire. Also out of the midst thereof came the likeness of four living creatures. And this was there appearance; they had the likeness of a man. And every one had four faces, and every one had four wings. And their feet were straight feet; and the sole of their feet was like the sole of a calf's foot: and they sparkled as the colour of burnished brass. And they had the hands of a man under their wings on their four sides; and they four had their faces and their wings. Their wings were joined one to another; they turned not when they went; they went every one straight forward. As for the likeness of their faces, they four had the face of a man, and the face of a lion, on the right side: and they four had the face of an ox on the left side; they four also had the face of an eagle. Thus were their faces: and their wings were stretched upward; two wings of every one were joined one to another, and two covered their bodies. And they went every one straight forward: whither the spirit was to go, they went; and they turned not when they went. As for the likeness of the living creatures, their appearance was like burning coals of fire, and like the appearance

of lamps: it went up and down among the living
creatures; and the fire was bright, and out of the
fire went forth lightning. And the living creatures
ran and returned as the appearance of a flash of
lightning. Now as I beheld the living creatures, behold
one wheel upon the earth by the living creatures, with
his four faces. The appearance of the wheels and their
work was like unto the colour of a beryl: and they four
had one likeness: and their appearance and their work
was as it were a wheel in the middle of a wheel. When
they went, they went upon their four sides: and they
turned not when they went. As for their rings, they
were so high that they were dreadful; and their rings
were full of eyes round about them four. And when
the living creatures went, the wheels went by them:
and when the living creatures were lifted up from
the earth, the wheels were lifted up. Whithersoever
the spirit was to go, they went, thither was their spirit
to go; and the wheels were lifted up over against
them: for the spirit of the living creature was in the
wheels. When those went, these went; and when those
stood, these stood; and when those were lifted up
from the earth, the wheels were lifted up over against
them: for the spirit of the living creature was in the
wheels. And the likeness of the firmament upon the
heads of the living creature was as the colour of
the terrible crystal, stretched forth over their heads
above. And under the firmament were their wings
straight, the one toward the other: every one had two,
which covered on this side, and every one had two,
which covered on that side, their bodies. And when
they went, I heard the noise of their wings, like the

noise of great waters, as the voice of the Almighty, the voice of speech, as the noise of an host: when they stood, they let down their wings. And there was a voice from the firmament that was over their heads, when they stood, and had let down their wings. And above the firmament that was over their heads was the likeness of a throne, as the appearance of a sapphire stone: and upon the likeness of the throne was the likeness as the appearance of a man above upon it. And I saw as the colour of amber, as the appearance of fire round about within it, from the appearance of his loins even upward, and from the appearance of his loins even downward, I saw as it were the appearance of fire, and it had brightness round about. As the appearance of the bow that is in the cloud in the day of rain, so was the appearance of the brightness round about. This was the appearance of the likeness of the glory of the LORD. And when I saw it, I fell upon my face, and I heard a voice of one that spake. Then the spirit took me up, and I heard behind me a voice of a great rushing, saying, Blessed be the glory of the LORD from his place. I heard also the noise of the wings of the living creatures that touched one another, and the noise of a great rushing. So the spirit lifted me up and took me away, and I went in bitterness, in the heat of my spirit; but the hand of the LORD was strong upon me."

You might wonder, why have we written this Book? What does it serve? Yes you might say, you have shown that white people are Cain's off spring. Yes, you might say, you have shown that white people's basic nature is to murder. Yes, you might say, you have shown that white people's whiteness of skin is a curse from the Almighty God. Yes, you might say, white people perfected lying, even lying to the Almighty God. Yes, you might say, you have shown that white people have a tendency toward taking what is not their own. Yes, you might say, you have shown that white people have a strong tendency to steal. Yes, you might say, you have shown that the God Almighty has said some very critical and demeaning things about white people. Yes, you might say, you have revealed that the Almighty God has said that no white people were saved in Biblical times. Yes, you might say, you have pointed out that very few of the white people will be in the first resurrection, the so-called rapture. Yes, you might say, you have shown that white people have mastered the practice of witchcraft and have prospered because it. Yes, you might say, Yes, Yes, Yes, you have shown, you have revealed, you have pointed out, but what is the value of it all. Why write the Book? First of all, we write the Book because God Almighty told us to. Secondly, we write the Book to fulfill the Scriptures written by Apostle John and Apostle Matthew of the New Testament of the Holy Scriptures/Bible.

John Ch. 8, V. 32

"And ye shall know the truth and the truth shall make you free."

Matthew Ch. 10, V. 26

"...for there is nothing covered that shall not be revealed: and hid that shall not be known."

You might ask, why would God want to make it known? Well, God in his wisdom to make it known, frees the world of the witchcraft over all of non-white mankind. White people through its witchcraft have made all the world to desire to be like them; to be like them even in the curse of their skin color. Yes, they have made a curse from God in the frailness of their skin color to be something to be desired. How great has been their witchcraft. Very few on this earth have not wanted the paleness of skin like white folks. The slaves taken from Africa by white folks, pale people, to the Americas, were made, through the mind control witchcraft, to strive to get rid of all the Blackness of their skin that was possible. This mind control witchcraft was carried out through a process called natural selection. All would seek and strive to get rid of the Blackness of their skin through breeding of having children with a white person, pale person or lighter complexion person.

For those who achieved/accomplished to become of a lighter complexion, they were rewarded by allowing them a better status in their captivity or oppression. In the case of slavery in the United States, the slaves were allowed to serve their so-called masters in his house. Other forms of this reward system was carried out also through other means. Always, however, the lighter your complexion, the better it was for you. This selection, this discrimination, eventually had the desired effect that the slave master wanted. The Black people wanted to look white/pale. This in turn would cause them not to or diminish the captives rising up against the slave master because they wanted to be like him. The mind control witchcraft would have had its desired effect. Refer to our Book, "God Said Black People In The United States Are Jews". Also, refer to an expected upcoming Book with the Title "I Use To Be An Uncle Tom". We will not reveal the Author's name at this time. All of the above of this mind control witchcraft was what God was indicating would happen from the very beginning in Genesis Chapter 4.

Genesis Ch. 4, Vs. 6 & 7

"And the LORD said unto Cain, Why art thou wroth? And why art thou contenance fallen? And if thou doest well, shalt thou not be accepted? And if thou doest not well, sin lieth at the door. <u>And unto thee shall be his desire, and thou shall rule over him.</u>"

The United States, Cuba, Mexico, Dominican Republic, Brazil, Columbia, Chilli, Venezuela, Haiti, Guatemala, Virgin Island, Bahamas and others of the Americas, were all witchcraft to rid themselves of the Blackness of their skin. Satan and white people made a curse from God to be something that is desired. Incredible! Absolutely Incredible!

Not only did Black and non-Black Jews strive to look white/pale, but others of the world also obsession was to be more white/pale looking. Yes, God told us from the very beginning that it would happen. The reason it has taken so long to understand this mind control witchcraft, lies also in the Holy Scriptures.

Matthew Ch. 10, V. 26

"…for there is nothing covered that shall not be revealed; and hid that shall not be known."

Genesis Ch. 4, V. 7

"…And unto thee shall be his desire, an thou shall rule over him."

Daniel Ch. 12, Vs. 8 & 9

"And I heard, but I understood not: then said I, O my lord, what shall be the ends of these things? And he said, Go thy way, Daniel: for the words are closed up and sealed to the time of the end."

The reason it has taken so long for this mind control witchcraft to be broken is because of God's people, the Jews, Black and non-Black, continual disobedience to God's word. God saw from the very beginning to the end what his people would do and, therefore, God could say the words that he said. God used Satan, through Cain's off spring, pale people, white people, to have most of his people to desire a curse and to have Cain's off spring, white people, pale people, to rule over them because of their disobedience. Not all of God's people disobeyed him, but most of them did.

Skin color and associated facial features were not the only things that the world and even some of God's people tried to imitate of white people, pale people. They also tried to imitate their life style and culture. Satan smiled. Satan's Plan for Mankind was really taking shape. This is why that you see the whole world taking on the culture of Cain's off spring, white folks, pale people. Refer to our Books:

1. "The Whole World Becoming As Sodom"

2. "Words From God, By God Appearing To Us Or Just Talking To Us, For The End Times"

3. "March Was When JESUS Was Born And Not Christmas"

4. "God Said Black People In The United States Are Jews"

Remember this, as we mentioned earlier, one of the names that represent the United States that is in the Holy Scriptures of the New Testament is Sodom. So, Cain's off spring, pale people, white people, are also known for sodomy/homosexuality. This is the life style that the whole world is trying to imitate. Refer to our Books:

1. "The Whole World Becoming As Sodom"

2. "Words From God, By God Appearing To Us Or Just Talking To Us, For The End Times"

3. "March Was When JESUS Was Born And Not Christmas"

Revelation Ch. 11, Vs. 3,7 & 8

"And I will give power unto my two witnesses...And when they shall have finished their testimony, the beast...shall overcome them, and kill them. And their dead bodies shall lie in the street of the great city, which spiritually is called Sodom…"

God warned his people in the Holy Scriptures/Bible not to imitate the heathen.

<u>Jeremiah Ch. 10, Vs. 1 & 2</u>

"Hear ye the word which the LORD speaketh unto you, O house of Israel: Thus saith the LORD, Learn not the way of the heathen…"

<u>I Kings Ch. 14, V. 24</u>

"And there were also sodomites in the land: and they did according to all the abominations of the nations which the LORD cast out before the children of Israel."

Now you know, one of the main reasons why God had Israel to kill the people in Biblical days/times; it was because they were sodomites/homosexuals. This is also one of the reasons why God will have the United States destroyed.

Starting with Former President Bill Clinton's Administration, the United States passed a law, that if you speak certain things against a homosexual/sodomite, it would be a crime. The elevation of them, the homosexuals/sodomites, were carried to a higher level during Former President George W. Bush's Administration. Even though during his Administration his Party, the Republicans, had control over everything; the Presidency, the House of Representatives, the Senate and Supreme Court.

Yet, laws were passed in certain States giving civil liberties to sodomites/homosexuals and their partners. The height of immorality, sin, reached its despicable and repugnant low under President Barack Obama's Presidency. Well, during President Barack Obama's Administration, homosexuals/sodomites reached one of their main goals. A president, President Barack Obama, declared that it should be the law of the land that homosexuals/sodomites should be given the official seal of approval by the Government to marry in all of the states of the United States. The United States' Supreme Court recently, during the writing of this Book, ruled on a case that essentially gave the stamp of approval by the United States officially recognizing sodomites/homosexuals to marry.

Although the last three Presidents have overtly done things to promote homosexuality/sodomy, as we have written before, all of the Presidents from George Washington to Barack Obama have been sodomites. Refer to our Books:

1. "The Whole World Becoming As Sodom"

2. "Words From God, By God Appearing To Us Or Just Talking To Us, For The End Times"

3. "The Judgment Of The United States"

In this day and time we would call the First President of the United States, George Washington, and those of that day, transvestites. A transvestite is a man who dresses up as a woman and a woman who dresses up as a man. George Washington and the other men of that day wore wigs. They also wore skirts. They also wore panty hoses. They also wore ruffles on their shirts as women wore and do wear. The men also shaved their face to be naked as a woman.

All of the immediate above paragraphs, just validates the word God; a word spoken by God (2,000) two thousand years ago. The United States is the modern day Sodom.

Also, the United States destiny with sodomy/ homosexuality is revealed by taking a close look at Egypt of old as being the spiritual equivalent of the United States. Sodomy/homosexuality was so prevalent in Egypt of old, until marriage between man and woman was such a rarity, until the reproduction of Egyptians was so low, that the children of Israel out-numbered them. Only (70) seventy of the children of Israel came to out-number the whole of Egypt.

Exodus Ch. 1, Vs. 7-9

"And the children of Israel were fruitful, and increased abundantly, and multiplied, and waxed exceeding mighty; and the land was filled with them. Now there arose up a new king over Egypt, which knew not Joseph. And he said unto his people, Behold, the people of the children of Israel are more and mightier than we…"

Why did sodomites/homosexuals become hypocrites? Why did they want to hide being a sodomite/ homosexual? This is a result of one main thing. This is a result of sodomites/homosexuals taking on the title of Christians. This happened with the emergence of the man in Rome winning the power struggle to be over the Church when Apostle John died. This emergence of control over, the then perverted Church by the man in Rome, he to eventually be called the Pope, made it impossible to be known as a sodomite at the same time calling yourself a Christian. Thus, the deceit was born. Thus, being a hypocrite of who you are was born. It was just too much written in the word of God against being a sodomite to hide or overlook.

Genesis Ch. 18, V. 20

"And the LORD said, Because the cry of Sodom and Gomorrah is great, and because their sin is very grievous..."

Genesis Ch. 19, Vs. 1,12 & 13

"And their came two angels to Sodom...And the men said unto Lot...we will destroy this place, because the cry of them is waxen great before the face of the LORD; and the LORD hath sent us to destroy it."

Leviticus Ch. 18, V. 22

"Thou shalt not lie with mankind, as with womankind: it is abomination."

Leviticus Ch. 18, V. 27

"(For all these abominations...the land is defiled:)"

Romans Ch. 1, Vs. 24-29 & 32

"Wherefore God also gave them up to uncleanness through the lusts of their own hearts…Who changed the truth of God into a lie…For this cause God gave them up into vile affections: for even their women did change the natural use into that which is against nature: And likewise also the men, leaving the natural use of the woman, burned in their lust one toward another; men with men working that which is unseemly, and receiving in themselves that recompense of their error was meet. And even as they did not like to retain God in their knowledge, God gave them up to a reprobate mind…Being filled with all unrighteousness… Who knowing the judgment of God, that they which commit such things are worthy of death, not only do the same, but have pleasure in them that do them."

This so-called Christian identity of the sodomites/ homosexuals had to happen because the (Anti- Christ) Beast had to come forth in the end times from the so-called Christians. The Former Pope, Pope John Paul II, Carol Josef Wojtyla, will be the so-called (Anti-Christ) Beast.

The off spring of Cain, white folks, pale people, have perfected lying. They have trained their society to lie by what they call acting. They even reward the best liar with a golden stature called the Oscar.

<u>John Ch. 8, V. 44</u>

"<u>Ye are of your father the devil,</u> and the lusts of
your father ye will do. He was a murderer from the
beginning, and abode not in the truth, because <u>there is
no truh in him.</u> When he speaketh a lie, he speaketh
of his own: <u>for he is a liar, and the father of it</u>."

Think about this, Cain's off spring, pale people,
white folks, reward the best liar/actor/actress with
a golden stature called the Oscar. What makes this
any different than idol god worshippers of old? They
are no different than those mentioned in the Holy
Scriptures/Bible and that which was written about the
pagans.

There are some good white folks. There are some of
the off spring of Cain, pale people, white folks, who
are good. Likewise, there are some who are not Cain's
off spring who are bad. You might from all that has
been written thus far, ask how could this be? You
might wonder, how could there be any good white
folks? It can be so, because God is in control.

<u>Proverbs Ch. 21, V. 1</u>

"THE king's heart is in the hand of the LORD, as the
rivers of water: he turneth it withersoever he will."

<u>Psalm 24, V. 1</u>

"The earth is the LORD's, and the fullness thereof;
the world, and they that dwell therein."

An example of God turning the king's heart for what God wanted him to do, can be seen when God caused the Pharaoh to promote Joseph, a slave, to be over all of Egypt. The Pharaoh made Joseph to be second in power to himself.

Genesis Ch. 37, V. 28

"…and they drew and lift up Joseph out of the pit, and sold Joseph to the Ishmeelites for twenty pieces of silver: and they brought Joseph into Egypt."

Genesis Ch. 41, Vs. 39-44

"And Pharaoh said unto Joseph, Forasmuch as God hath shewed thee all this, there is none so discreet and wise as thou art: Thou shalt be over my house, and according unto thy word shall all my people be ruled: only in the throne will I be greater than thou. And Pharaoh said unto Joseph, See, I have set the over all the land of Egypt. And Pharaoh took off his ring from his hand, and put it upon Joseph's hand, and arrayed him in vestures of fine linen, and put a golden chain about his neck; And he made him to ride in the second chariot which he had: and they cried before him, Bow the knee: and he made him ruler over all the land of Egypt. And Pharaoh said unto Joseph, I am Pharaoh, and without thee shall no man lift up his hand or foot in all the land of Egypt."

Yes, you might say, but that was in Biblical days. You might say, God does not do any like that now. Well, consider this. President Barack Obama an off spring of slaves of the United States, defeated a white man for the Presidency who is one of the riches men in the world, the riches ever to run for the Presidency. President Barack Obama defeated Mitt Romney. This only could have happen if the controversial "Obama Care" was ruled to be legal by the United States' Supreme Court. The United States' Supreme Court is and was control during the Presidential Election by Mitt Romney's main Republican supporters. The Justices of the Supreme Court was evenly split and only the Chief Justice could break the tie; Chief Justice John Roberts. Chief Justice John Roberts is and was during the Presidential Election a great enemy/opponent of President Barack Obama. His bitterness toward President Barack Obama was and is so great that he fumble an age old custom and duty of the Chief Justice of swearing in Barack Obama to be President during his first term in office. Now for the second term to determine the Presidency; here comes the Chief Justice's vote on "Obama Care", with the whole world watching, and Mitt Romney and the Republicans already celebrating. Chief Justice John Roberts voted for "Obama Care", thereby, delivering the Presidency to Barack Obama.

I know that Chief Justice John Roberts is having many sleepless nights wondering why he voted that way. Let us give you some rest. The king's heart as well as the Chief Justice heart are in the hand of the LORD, as the rivers of water, HE turneth it withersoever HE will.

The Chief Justice, John Roberts, was so mad, so disgusted, so outraged, with his vote on "Obama

Care" which delivered the Presidential Election to President Barack Obama, that he gutted the Voting Rights Act which helped Black people. Little does he know, God will also use this to help Black people.

So, we see no matter what Satan has planned for Cain's off spring, pale people, white folks, God can still/yet do what he wants. God said he will have mercy on whoever he desires.

<u>Romans Ch. 9, V. 15</u>

"For he saith to Moses, I will have mercy on whom I will have mercy, and I will have compassion on whom I will have compassion."

There are some good white folks. God let us know that there are even some white folks that will be saved. Although very few of the very few, some will be saved. Some will be in the First Resurrection, the so-called rapture. God even prophesied through my wife, Prophetess Sylvia Franklin, some years ago, that there will be some white folks under my Apostleship. God showed that one of them will be a very famous woman who is known throughout the earth. God showed me, also some years ago, that I will be laying hands on people anointing them with gifts to go and minister. Among them were a few white people.

Let us say this. Not all at this point in time of Cain's off spring are sodomites/homosexuals. There are a few who are not. Refer to our Books:

1. "The Whole World Becoming As Sodom"

2. "Words From God, By God Appearing To Us Or Just Talking To Us, For The End Times"

Let us say a few words about this. It has been said by most of sodomites/homosexuals that they were born that way. The life style of those involved in sodomy/homosexuality is a sin. All sin is from Satan. The person who chooses this life style chooses to sin. Those who are sodomites/homosexuals have been possessed by Satan or demons/evil spirits. If sodomites/homosexuals have children their babies and children are possessed by Satan or demons/evil spirits. So, it goes on and on, generation after generation. There is one way for this chain to be broken. The sodomite/homosexual MUST be born again. The person MUST be filled with Holy Ghost/Spirit and get baptized in the name of JESUS. When you are filled with the Holy Ghost/Spirit you speak in tongues as the Spirit gives the utterance. When you are baptized you MUST be baptized in the name of JESUS. Both are essential to be delivered from this sodomy/homosexuality and to stay delivered. Later on in this Book we provide four easy steps on how to get delivered and to stay delivered; to be born again. Refer to our Books:

1. "The Whole World Becoming As Sodom"

2. "Words From God, By God Appearing To Us Or Just Talking To Us, For The End Times"

Not only is the above, the only way for Cain's off spring to be delivered from sodomy/homosexuality, but also all others; Black people and all non-Cain's off spring.

Although a sodomite/homosexual is an abomination to God, there is, however, someone who is worse than that in God's eye sight. The worst to God that is on this earth is in great abundance. The worst, even worse than a sodomite/homosexual, is one who rejects God's word. Look at what God said in the Holy Scriptures/Bible in the New Testament. Refer to Matthew Chapter 10, Verses 14 & 15.

<u>Matthew Ch. 10, Vs. 14 & 15</u>

"And whosoever shall not receive you, nor hear your words, when ye depart out of that house or city, shake off the dust off your feet. Verily I say unto you, It shall be more tolerable for the land of Sodom and Gomorarrha in the day of judgment, than for that city."

Consider this however. What would be God's view of a sodomite/homosexual who rejects God's word.

It seems like whatever God said not to do, Satan has caused man to do it. It seems like whatever God has said that is filthy and not to touch, Satan has had man to touch. It seems like whatever God has told man not to do, Satan has man doing it. Whatever God has said in his word, the Scriptures, Satan has perverted through his children, including Cain's off spring.

God loves all of his natural creation, but God expects his particular creation to function as God intended. For instance, God told man to dominate his other natural creation on earth. God did not expect a worm or cat or dog or bird or lizard, etc., to rule over man.

<u>Genesis Ch. 1, Vs. 26-28</u>

"And God said, Let us make man in our image, after our likeness: and let them have dominion over the fish of the sea, and over the fowl of the air, and over the cattle, and over all the earth, and over every creeping thing that creepeth upon the earth. So God created man in his own image, in the image of God created him; male and female created he them. And God bless them, and said unto them, Be fruitful, and multiply, and replenish the earth and subdue it: and have dominion over the fish of the sea, and over the fowl of the air, and over every living thing that moveth upon the earth."

So, God expects none of his other natural creation on earth to be like man. God never expects a dog, cat or whatever to be like man. A dog has his place; a cat has his place; a bird has his place; etc. has his place. Satan, however, has man having so-called pets; even pets that live in man's house; even pets that sleep in his/her bed; even pets that man has sex with. Having pets such as dogs and cats in the house is animal abuse. Those who do these things say that they are showing love for animals, but actually it is the opposite. God made a dog to roam free. God made a cat to roam free. God made a dog and a cat to be free to hunt for their food. To be free to choose a mate. To be free to give birth. To be free to fight or to run. All of these things makes the dog and cat whole; what they are supposed to be. Man with his fake love, has, however, imprisoned the dog and cat. Man has robbed the beast from the dog and cat. Man has even rendered much of the species of the dog and cat of the ability to reproduce. Man call it spading and neutering. What cruelty! What Selfishness! For your pleasure, you rod another of its pleasure. The pleasure of the beast to roam free and reproduce. Then, you, man, hypocritically, say that you love animals. Then after all of this, you then pervert the dog and cat by having sex with them. Cain! Cain! Cain!

In the case of a dog, God has indicated that a dog is a filthy beast. A beast that should be undesirable for habitation with man.

Exodus Ch. 11, V. 7

"But against any of the children of Israel shall not a dog move his tongue, against man or beast: that ye may know that the LORD doth put a difference between the Egyptians and Israel."

Deuteronomy Ch. 23, V. 18

"Thou shalt not bring the hire of a whore, or the price of a dog, into the house of the LORD thy God for any vow: for even both these are abomination unto the LORD thy God."

Proverbs Ch. 26, V. 11

"As a dog returneth to his vomit, so a fool returneth to his folly."

Luke Ch. 16, Vs. 19-20

"There was a certain rich man, which was clothed in purple and fine linen, and fared sumptuously every day: and there was a certain beggar named Lazarus, which was laid at his gate, full of sores, And desiring to be fed with the crumbs which fell from the rich man's table: moreover the dogs came and licked his sores."

Revelation Ch. 22, Vs. 14 & 15

"Blessed are they that do his commandment, that they may have right to the tree of life, and may enter in through the gates into the city. For without are dogs, and sorceries, and whoremongers, and murderers, and idolaters, and whosoever loveth and maketh a lie."

Whether God is referring to the dog himself or referring to a man as a dog, it is a demeaning statement. How many of white folks, pale people, Cain's off spring, have dogs and cats in their house? How many of white folks, pale people, Cain's off spring, have dogs and cats in their bed? How many of white folks, pale people, Cain's off spring, have dogs and cats licking their face and mouth?

Cain's off spring, white folks, pale people, also have some of the rest of Mankind imitating them regarding dogs and cats. After learning these things which we have written what God says about dogs and cats, will Cain's off spring, white folks, pale people, repent of their filthy ways? We think not. Now you can understand, even another reason why so very few of

Cain's off spring, white folks, pale people, will be saved; will be in the First Resurrection, the so-called rapture.

The filthy part, sex with animals, of Cain's off spring's, white folk's, pale people, culture is beastality. Not all have drop to this low, but nearly all are headed this way. Beastality is a man or woman having sex with an animal. The obsession of Cain's off spring, white folks, pale people, having pets living in their house is the path to this abomination. Satan will cause it to happen. Satan is filthy. During these last days, the end times, will be a time on the earth when all sins that ever was will be manifested. Beastality was done in days of old and is/will be done in this day.

Exodus Ch. 22, V. 19

"Whosoever lieth with a beast shall surely be put to death."

Leviticus Ch. 18, V. 23

"Neither shalt thou lie with any beast to defile thyself therewith: neither shall any woman stand before a beast to lie down thereto: it is confusion."

Leviticus Ch. 20, Vs. 15 & 16

"And if any man lie with a beast, he shall surely be put to death: and ye shall slay the beast. And if any woman approach unto any beast, and lie down thereto, thou shall kill the woman and the beast: they shall surely be put to death; their blood shall be upon them."

<u>Deuteronomy Ch. 27, V. 21</u>

"Cursed be he that lieth with any manner of beast…"

Let us be clear. We and you should not kill people in this day and time. We are under a New Covenant with God. If there is any killing done for unrighteousness, God himself will do it. It is even against the law to kill an animal in the United States. This law was passed during Former President George W. Bush's time in office.

If beastality was not being done, then God would not have had so much to say about it. As the end of time approaches, immorality and sin are increasing.

When I was a sinner, in my middle to latter (20's) twenties, while living in Cleveland, Ohio of the United States, I often went to bars or night clubs. One evening as I entered a bar, a porno movie was being showed in there. I, a seasoned sinner, was shocked. I had never seen such before. White folks, pale people, men and women, were having sex with animals. It almost made me vomit. They were having sex with cows, horses, dogs, goats, hogs, chickens and maybe some other animals; including oral sex; the people performing oral sex on the animals. These were people who looked like anybody you might see on the job, in the store or church. After viewing this pornography, I was never the same again. I was a whoremonger, but I could not have sex for about two weeks. Every time I would see a white person, I would think of them having sex with an animal. Every time I would see a white person with a pet, I thought of them having sex with the animal. The above happened in the early (70's) seventies. That was about (40) forty years ago. How much more is the abomination now.

The Almighty God is a good God. The Almighty God is the good God. In spite of being the off spring of Cain and all that this implies, God will yet allow a few of the enemies of his people to be saved. If they repent of their evil, they yet can be saved like all others who will be saved. All MUST repent and get born again and obey God's word. All MUST speak in tongues as God give the utterance and get baptized in the name of JESUS for the remission of their sins and obey God's word to be saved. Refer to our Book "The Door Is Closing On The Last Opportunity For Immortality".

Not many white people, Cain's off spring, pale people, will be saved. Will you be among the few who will be saved? Or will you lie to yourself as normally has been the case as Cain's off spring, pale people, white folks, and go to hell and burn in the lake of fire.

Let us be clear. For those of us who do not have Cain's mark, non-white people, we also MUST be born again and obeys God's words to be saved; to be in the First Resurrection, the so-called rapture.

Yes, the Almighty God, the Creator of the Universe, is a good God; the good God. God is the merciful

God. However, make no mistake, God will avenge his people; just like in days of old; eventually it will happen. Since the world is coming to an end, this eventuality is soon to happen. Yes, there is the judgment of the very few of the very few of the off spring of Cain being in the First Resurrection, the so-called rapture, but, also, there is a natural judgment that must take place. It will happen soon. So says God.

You might wonder/ask, if God punished his people for disobedience by having Cain's off spring, white people, pale people, to rule over them, then why would Cain's off spring, pale people, white folks, be judged by God? The answer to this is in the Scriptures. God said what you sow, you reap. God also indicated that he might use you to do evil, but you will have pay for that evil.

Galatians Ch. 6, V. 7

"Be not deceived; God is not mocked: for whatsoever a man soweth, that shall he also reap."

Matthew Ch. 18, V. 7

"Woe unto the world because of offenses: for it must needs be that offenses come; but woe to that man by whom the offense come."

Judas Iscariot committed an offense against JESUS. JESUS chose him to do it, but Judas had to pay for the offense of betraying JESUS. It was even prophesied many hundreds of years before it happened that Judas would have to pay for his betrayer.

Psalm 109, Vs. 6-8

"… let Satan stand at his right hand. When he shall he shall be judged, let him be condemned: and let his prayer become sin. Let his days be few; and let another take his office."

Acts Ch. 1, Vs. 16-20

"Men and brethren, this scripture must needs have been fulfilled, which the Holy Ghost by the mouth of David spake before concerning Judas, which was guide to them which took Jesus. For he was numbered with us, and had obtained part of this ministry. Now this man purchased a field with the reward of iniquity, and falling headlong, he burst asunder in the midst, and all his bowels gushed out. And it was known unto all the dwellers at Jerusalem; insomuch as that field is called in their proper tongue, Aceldama, that is to say, The field of blood. For it is written in the book of Psalm, Let his habitation be desolate, and let no man dwell therein: and his bishoprick let another take."

You must know, when it comes to his people, God will avenge them. Even though God prophesied to Abraham that Israel would go into captivity in Egypt for (400) four hundred years, God yet punished Egypt for the offense."

The main purpose of this Book is to break the power of witchcraft of Cain's off spring, white folks, pale people, off of the rest of this world. Witchcraft's power is in deceit. This Book sets the world free of the deceit that Cain's off spring, white folks, pale people, are something special or superior and therefore, should be imitated. A deficiency/ frailness/curse is not a characteristic of superiority. We have given you the truth regarding Cain' off spring, white people, pale people. What the world has been bewitched to believe is a shameful deceit. A perversion of the truth is what the world has been bewitched with.

<u>John Ch. 8, V. 32</u>

"And ye shall know the truth, and the truth shall make you free."

We end these writings regarding Cain's Mark with this. Cain's mark will eventually lead to the 666 Mark of the (Anti-Christ) Beast. The 666 Mark of the (Anti-Christ) Beast will be based on money and who is in control. Pope John Paul II, Carol Josef Wojtyla, will be the (Anti-Christ) Beast. That old devil is not dead. He is alive and living in the Vatican. God himself has told and shown us this. Former President Bill Clinton will administer evil on behalf of the (Anti-Christ) Beast. Former President Bill Clinton is the other beast, the False Prophet. God himself has told and shown us this. Refer to our Books:

1. "The Name Of The (Anti-Christ) Beast And 666 Identification"

2. "Who Is The (False Prophet) Second Beast"

The wisdom of God, how great it is. God needed Cain and his off spring, white folks, pale people, to complete his Plan for the <u>redemption</u> of Mankind.

God used Satan to complete his Plan for Mankind. Again, even again, God made a fool out of Satan. Even again, Satan thinking himself to be slick, God makes a fool out of him. God makes a fool out of Satan to make sure that his', God's, Plan for Mankind is perfected.

Satan is nothing. Allow me this time of delight and to mock Satan. We have written of this in our Book "God Tells How To Eliminate Famine", but allow this pleasure/enjoyment again for me. [In the beginning of the Year we called 2012, GOD showed me how Satan looks and of his limits. GOD had shown me Satan (3) three or (4) four times in the past, but it was a silhouette form of Satan. In the beginning of the Year we called 2012, GOD allowed me to see in detail how Satan looks. GOD was walking with me, I believe it was GOD, it might have been an angel. We were walking toward the east. We walked up to a wall. A brick wall about (4) four feet high. The wall was at the top of an inclining area of a far distance. GOD let me know that this was Satan's territory. All of a sudden Satan came running up the incline toward us. He was loudly saying that we had no business there. At that moment a hatred came upon me against Satan like I had never experienced before. I then jumped over the wall where Satan was and began to beat him. I choked him. I beat him in his face. I kicked him. I stomped him. I squeezed him. I slapped him. I did these things over and over again. Satan was not able to do anything to me. I finally realized that I could not kill him. I then left him along and got back on the other side of the wall. He was laying down there like a whipped dog. I can tell you exactly how he looked. He was about (6) six feet to (6) six feet and (2) inches tall. He was not overweight and he was not skinny. He looked the age of a man in his forties or fifties. He looked like a white man with a tan. The shape of his head reminds you of Mitt Romney. GOD showed me this to let me know that Satan is nothing! Satan is nothing to be feared! GOD let me beat the " snot " out of Satan to show me this. Satan has deceived some of mankind to build him up before human beings so that we as human beings will think that he is something to be feared! He is nothing! Satan is nothing! GOD, also, showed me this about Satan, to let me know that I had the victory over Satan. Some of mankind through its witchcraft/magic, divination, sorcery, make Satan look like he is something. Satan through his wizards/warlocks, witches and witchcraft workers make Satan look like he is something.]

These ministers and worshippers of Satan make him out to be something so great, but he is nothing! Just look at what will be said of Satan when the truth is finally realized. They will mock him.

Isaiah Ch. 14, Vs. 16 & 17

"…Is this the man…?"

APOSTLE FREDERICK E. FRANKLIN'S TESTIMONY

Let me give you my personal testimony. Let me tell you about how I got filled with the Holy Ghost. Back in 1985 I lived in Washington, D.C. I was not married at that time. It was in October of 1985. I had my own business as a Utilities Engineering Consultant. As a sinner and as usually was the case, I left out of a certain bar around 1:00 am. When finally I reached the place where I was living and was opening my door, the telephone began to ring. I went in and answered the telephone. It was my first cousin calling from Mobile, Alabama. He, also, was about high and was just getting in from a bar. As usually was the case, we started talking about God. We knew little to nothing about God, but somehow we always started talking about God. As we talked, I started talking about the preachers of God. I said that those O lying preachers that say they lay hands on people and they get healed are the worst ones. I said only Jesus could heal someone like that. I at least knew that Jesus could heal like that. My cousin said you are right. Two drunks talking. He then said the only other ones who could do that were Peter, John, Paul and the other Apostles of the Holy Bible. I was shocked. I was so shocked that I got sober. I said what! What! He said yes! Peter, John, Paul and the other Apostles laid hands on the people and they got healed. I was totally astounded! I was totally amazed! I was sober!

After we hanged up the telephone, I went and picked up the Bible which I had kept with me since about 1963. I had never opened the Bible I was just religious and kept it with me. I had been putting off reading it for all these years. When the urge would come to me to read it, I would put it off to the next month, or next week, or next day, or when I finished a certain project, or when I finished during this or that. I did not know it then, but I know now, the urge was God trying to get me to read the Bible. I finally dusted off and opened that Bible. It was now around 2:00 am. I wanted to see for myself where it said that a man could lay hands on a person and he or she could get healed. I was after all, an Electrical Engineer and this was illogical. How could flesh, blood and bones heal someone? It did not make any sense. Not having any idea where to look, I searched and searched and searched. I read and read and read. Finally, somewhere between 3:00-4:00 am, I found it. I saw that Peter laid hands on people and they got healed. It was amazing! It was like a very bright light was turned on in my head. I was speechless. To understand the greatness of my astonishment, you need to understand my childhood hopelessness. I, as a child, being black brought up in Alabama, living far out in a rural area, started working when I was four years old. I would go outside of our house at night, walking through the woods, looking up in the sky at the moon and the stars, and ask God why? I knew it had to be a God. I would ask God why would he leave his children down on this earth at the mercy of Satan? Satan of course, I knew, had no mercy. I could not understand why. Everything that seemed to be good, appeared to be on Satan's side. The evil people had it. White folks had it who were doing evil. Why, why, why, was my question? I never received an answer. It appeared that God could care less about the suffering of and in justice to his children on this earth.

When I saw that someone could get healed by another just by laying hands on them, then I understood clearly the answer to my why. I understood that God had not left us at the mercy of Satan. I, however, wanted to see could anyone lay hands on people and they could get healed. As I continued to search and read, now about day break, I "discovered" that you had to have the Holy Ghost to be able to heal. I wanted then to see could anyone receive the Holy Ghost. Now far in the morning of the next day, I "discovered" that anyone could receive the Holy Ghost. I "discovered" that you spoke in tongues when you received the Holy Ghost. My life desire would never be the same again. I wanted to see how I could receive the Holy Ghost. I learned that you had to repent. So, I asked God to forgive my sins. Then I asked God to give me the Holy Ghost, let me speak in tongues. Nothing happened. I did not speak in tongues. All that day I was asking God to forgive my sins and to let me speak in tongues. I did not work that day. This went on all day and into the night. Nothing ever happened. Exhausted I fell asleep into the next morning. When I woke the next day I started doing the same thing. I asked God to forgive my sins and let me speak in tongues. Nothing happened. I thought that maybe I need to read God's word and then I might receive the Holy Ghost. So, I read several Books of the Bible. Then I asked God to forgive my sins and let me speak in tongues. Nothing happened. I did this over and over each day and nothing ever happened. I had stop working all together. To receive the Holy Ghost was the most important thing in my life. I made a pledge to God that I would not go to the bars again. Nothing happened as I sought for the Holy Ghost. I made a pledge to God to stop drinking and stop smoking marijuana. Nothing happened. I made a pledge to God to stop fornicating. Nothing happened as I sought for the Holy Ghost. I was praying for the Holy Ghost and reading God's word and nothing happened. I decided to read the whole Bible. I read from Genesis through the Book of Revelation and nothing happened as I sought for the Holy Ghost during that time. Now it was the end of the year of 1985 and nothing happened as I sought for the Holy Ghost. I decided to move from Washington, D.C., back to my house in Montgomery, Alabama. Now after reading the whole Bible, I was praying about (22) twenty two hours a day to receive the Holy Ghost and nothing happened. I started crying and praying and nothing happened. I had only cried (4) four times in my life. I remember all the way back from (2) two years old. Crying and seeking for the Holy Ghost is all I did. I never spoke in tongues. This crying and seeking God for the Holy Ghost reached now into August of the year 1986. I had counted all of the months, weeks, and days to that time of seeking for the Holy

Ghost, now seeking about (22) twenty two hours a day. I had about (3) three months before, cleaned out my house of everything that I thought was sinful. I threw away all pornography, whiskey, wine and beer, marijuana and whatever I thought was sinful into my trash can. I did this and nothing ever happened. Now here it was in August, seeking to speak in tongues and I had not. I said, I thought, that maybe I need to join a Church. This might would help, I thought. I looked into the yellow pages of the phone book and chose (4) four churches that I would check out to join. This was now August 3, 1986. I was still seeking God for the Holy Ghost. I still was crying and praying to speak in tongues about (22) twenty two hours a day. On August 3, 1986, I turned on my television early in the morning and turning the channels I saw and heard some ridiculous sounding Church Choir singing with the TV camera shaking. I stopped to see what in the world would this be on television so unprofessional. I was amazed. I had once worked at a television station in Cleveland, Ohio, and I was just amazed at this. As I looked and listened in amazement, a young woman came before the camera to introduce/present her Apostle. She said that her Apostle laid hands on people, preformed many miracles and prayed for many to receive the Holy Ghost. This really caught my attention. I thought, could this be the answer to my quest? Then her Apostle came forth. A black, tall, old man, Apostle William A. Tumlin. I had already decided that I wanted to join a church under an old man who really knew something about God. Also, I wanted it to be a small church. I did not want anything to be like that Baptist Church that I was brought up in. All they cared about was looks, a big choir, a big church, a big funeral, always looks. They cared about looks, but yet certain ones was committing adultery and it seemed to be alright. Many were drunks and it seemed not to matter. I was brought up in this and had not learned hardly anything that I had finally read in the Bible.

Yet seeking God for the Holy Ghost, on August 10, 1986, I decided to first check out this Church and Apostle that I had seen on Television, before checking out the other churches. I went to the Church and it was a small church. I went into the Church and the Apostle preached and ask did anyone want to join the Church, I to my amazement went up and join the Church. I thought that the Apostle would pray for me to receive the Holy Ghost, but he did not. I was confused. After the service was dismissed, I went to the Apostle's wife and told her that I wanted to receive the Holy Ghost. She said, Oh, I thought you already had the Holy Ghost. She told me to go and tell the Apostle. I went to the Apostle and said I want to receive the Holy Ghost. He said Oh, I thought you already had the Holy Ghost. He said come back, either next Sunday or that afternoon before the 6:00 taping of the radio broadcast, and he would pray for me to receive the Holy Ghost. I said that I would come back before the taping of the broadcast. I was not about to wait for a whole week. I could tell you how many months, weeks and days I had been seeking for the Holy Ghost. I had been

seeking for the Holy Ghost every day
since October of 1985 and it was now
August 10, 1986.

When I went home from Apostle
Tumlin's Church, The All Nations Church
of God, I did something that was
key to me receiving the Holy Ghost.
Remember I told you that I threw away
all, pornography, whiskey, wine, beer,
marijuana and other things I thought
was sinful into my trash can. Well, I
went back to my trash can and I got
(2) two marijuana joints out of it and
brought them back into my house. I
had stop smoking marijuana during
my time of seeking the Holy Ghost
and had no intentions of smoking
anymore. I did not know it at that
time, but I know it now, it was Satan
that convinced me to get those (2) two
joints out of my trash can. I thought,
Satan told me, that I might need them
if I got a headache. I just had them in
my closet in case I might need them
for a headache. The Devil, Satan, just
made a fool out of me. The only time
I had those headaches is when I had
a hangover. I was not going to have a

hangover because I had stop drinking. What a fool. However, on August, 10, 1986, before I went back to receive the Holy Ghost, it had to be God who told me, I went to my closet and got those two joints and flushed them down my toilet stool. When I did this, it felt like a very, very, heavy weight was taken off me. At 5:00 on August 10, 1986, I was back at Apostle Tumlin's Church, The All Nations Church of God, to receive the Holy Ghost. I went in the Church and sat down in about the fourth row of the pews, next to the aisle, on the left side looking from the pulpit. There were about (3) three to (4) four people in the sanctuary, including the Apostle's wife. They were there praying. However, the Apostle was nowhere to be seen. I sat there waiting for the Apostle and he never showed up. It was now 5:30 pm and there was no sign of the Apostle. I was getting very anxious because the radio broadcast's taping was to start at 6:00 pm. Finally, the Apostle came out of a room from the front of the Church. I was so excited! I finally was going to receive the Holy Ghost! The Apostle walked towards me and down

the aisle and right by me and went into
the rest room near the entrance to
the Church. He did not say one word
to me. Not even a gesture toward me.
Some minutes past by and he was still
back there. I just kept praying. I just
kept repenting. Finally he came out.
He came to the back of me and put his
hands on my head and said receive the
Holy Ghost. I was excited and nervous.
I did not know what to expect. Then
with his hands on my head, he said
speak in tongues. I said to myself, what
is this man talking about? I said to
myself, you have to receive the Holy
Ghost before you speak in tongues. He,
the Apostle, just kept saying speak in
tongues. Then he, with hands on my
head, started speaking in tongues. Then
he said receive the Holy Ghost, speak
in tongues. Then he started speaking in
tongues. Then he said speak in tongues
with his hands on my head. Then to
my amazement he began to give up on
me and remove his hands, I stood up
so his hands could not be removed. I
thought to myself, no, no, you are not
going to give up on me this quick. So
he let his hands stay on my head and

began to speak in tongues. Then he said speak in tongues. I by this time, with the Apostle's hands on my head, was standing in front of the church facing the pews, but I did not know it. He said again speak in tongues. I said to myself this is not working, I am going to get out of here. I said to myself, the next time that he speaks in tongues I am just going to mimic him and pretend that I have the Holy Ghost so I can leave. He then spoke in tongues. Then I went to mimic him. The next thing I knew, I was speaking in a language that sounded like Hebrew, before the audience of people in the Church, motioning my hands like I was before them teaching them something. Then I said to myself, what in the world am I doing. This was totally unlike me. Then the Apostle said, you have been filled with the Holy Ghost. Then all of a sudden I stop speaking this Hebrew like language. The Apostle just kept saying you have been filled with the Holy Ghost. I was saying to myself, is this what it is to be filled with the Holy Ghost? I did not know what to say. I did not know what to think. I went

and sat back down in the same place
that I was sitting before. By this time,
it was time for the taping of the radio
broadcast. As I sat there, Satan began
to talk to me. He told me that I did not
have the Holy Ghost. He said that as
evil as I had been, that God would not
give me the Holy Ghost. Satan then
brought up to me every evil thing that
I had done. He kept saying, you do
not have the Holy Ghost. This went
on for about an hour as I sat there.
After the taping was over and I left the
Church, Satan kept up his accusations
and saying that I did not have the Holy
Ghost. All the way as I drove home,
he kept it up. When I entered into my
house I said to God that if I received
the Holy Ghost, let me know without a
shadow of doubt. Immediately I began
to speak in tongues. I was speaking
loud in tongues. I began to analyze this
speaking. I was not trying to mimic. My
mouth and tongue were moving and
I was not trying to make them move.
I was speaking sounding eloquently,
whatever I was speaking. This speaking
went on for about an hour with me
analyzing to see whether it was me

or God speaking. I then thought that I might not be able to stop speaking in tongues. Immediately I stop speaking in tongues and God spoke to me clearly and said that my name had been written in the Book of Life and everything has been worth it. I knew what God meant by worth it and I started crying. All of these months. All of these weeks. All of these days. All of the praying. All of the crying. All of this seeking for the Holy Ghost, but it is worth it. Later on I would get baptized by the Apostle in the name of Jesus Christ for the remission of my sins.

This one thing I want to point out. I could have received the Holy Ghost, all the way back in October of 1985, if I had got rid of that dope and the other things of sin. You cannot hold on to the past, anything of the past that is sin, and receive the Holy Ghost. Satan would have caused me to go to hell over (2) two marijuana joints. Two joints would have kept me from immortality.

PROPHETESS SYLVIA FRANKLIN'S TESTIMONIES OF RECEIVING THE HOLY GHOST

When my wife, Prophetess Sylvia Franklin, was a child she had a very depressing life. There was constant arguing and fighting between her father and mother. Her father would be drunk and pull out a gun and threaten to kill her mother and even at certain times to kill her and her brother.

At (10) ten years old, Sylvia would look out of her window and look up and ask God to take away the gloom and let the sun shine. She always would do this. It always seemed to be so gloomy in those days. As time went by in this constant state of family turmoil, at (13) thirteen years old, God did let the sun shine in Sylvia's life. After Sylvia, her mother and brother started attending a small Holiness Church, Sylvia was involved with a street meeting service. This was Apostle William Tumlin's Church. During the meeting the people were singing and praising the Lord.

Sylvia then started singing and praising the Lord and all of a sudden she started speaking in tongues.

Not really understanding what had happened to her, Sylvia was in and out of Church. As time passed Sylvia lost the Holy Ghost. At (17) seventeen years old Sylvia was in a service at Apostle William A. Tumlin's Church, All Nations Church of God. While singing and praising was taking place in the Church, Apostle Tumlin came to where Sylvia was and laid hands on her head and she started speaking in tongues. She was restored in the Holy Ghost. Later on she got baptized by Apostle Tumlin in the name of Jesus Christ for the remission of sins. Sylvia's life was never the same again.

OUR OLDEST CHILD ELIJAH JEREMIAH EZEKIEL FRANKLIN'S TESTIMONY OF RECEIVING THE HOLY GHOST

On January 31, 1995 our son, Elijah Jeremiah Ezekiel Franklin, had his fifth birthday. This is the same child the doctors said would have only a ten percent or less chance of being born. This is the same child some would have recommended being aborted (murdered in the womb). This is the same child who is in very good health. This is the same child the doctors said would have probable extreme health problems. This is the same child who was born premature.

After turning five years old, two days later on February 2, 1995, while we (Frederick and Sylvia) were praying for him in our house during our weekly Thursday night prayer service, he was filled with the Holy Ghost. He spoke in tongues for about an hour. After he finished speaking in tongues, we baptized him in the name of Jesus.

Through the testimony of Elijah's salvation, other children have desired to be saved and were indeed filled with the Holy Ghost and baptized in the name of Jesus.

NOTE THIS. Two Days After Elijah Spoke In Tongues, He Prophesied And Said, God Is Saying To Him, That We Would Be Moving To A Farm In Mobile, With Farm Animals. Later On That Year, In October, We Moved To That Farm.

DANIEL ISAIAH FRANKLIN'S AND REBEKAH ANNA FRANKLIN'S TESTIMONIES OF RECEIVING THE HOLY GHOST

This dedication is to give praise and glory to God Almighty, Father Jesus our Lord and Savior and to his Son Jesus Christ of whom the Father dwelled in on this earth, for the born again experience of Daniel Isaiah and Rebekah Anna.

June 15, 1998 was a special day in our family. This is the day that we completed household salvation in our family, the day that we could say that all five of us were born again. On this day, June 15, 1998, as we all prayed fervently during our daily dedicated afternoon prayer, God moved mightily in our presence. We were already excited for the young woman that we had prayed to receive the Holy Ghost the past night which we were preparing to baptize after our prayer time.

As we prayed fervently for God to move in a special way that day for the souls to be saved in our community, God spoke to us to pray for Daniel and Rebekah. We, Frederick, Sylvia and Elijah, started praying for them to be filled with the Holy Ghost. As we prayed, we noticed that Daniel and Rebekah were under the influence of the presence of God in praising him and they began to speak in tongues. We wondered could this actually be happening this fast as we had been praying for? Could our five year old son and four year old daughter now finally be filled with the Holy Ghost? We had been praying to God every day since they were conceived in Sylvia's womb for them to receive the Holy Ghost. We didn't really know whether they were speaking in tongues or not at this time because during prayer our children often would mimic us when we were speaking in tongues. But, this time seemed to be different, especially with Rebekah. Daniel Isaiah, every since he was about one year old, always has fervently praised the Lord, singing, dancing, lifting up his hands to God and appearing to speak in tongues.

Rebekah, however, did not normally praise God as enthusiastically as did Daniel. But on this day, June 15, 1998, at about 2:00 p.m., our little Rebekah was on fire! And even the normally enthusiastic Daniel seemed to have a double portion. We looked at them and wondered could this actually be it? Could our Daniel Isaiah be filled with the Holy Ghost? Could our son, who was born three months premature, be now born again of the Spirit? Could our son, who at one time only weighed (2) two pounds and (13) thirteen ounces, be born again of the Spirit? Could our son, who the doctors said would have to stay in the hospital for at least three months after he was born, who only stayed one month because he was so healthy, could he actually be speaking in tongues? Could this, our son who is strong and in excellent health who doctors said would have severe and numerous health problems, be born again of the Spirit? Could it also be that our little Rebekah be born again of the Spirit? Could it be that the Daddy's little girl, that he calls "Pretty Pretty" be born again of the Spirit? Could both

Daniel Isaiah and Rebekah be filled with the Holy Ghost? Could Frederick now release our second book for publication after waiting for Daniel and Rebekah to be born again so he could dedicate some pages in the book to their born again experience as he had done in our first with Elijah?

We did not want to make a mistake here and tell Daniel and Rebekah that they had been filled with the Holy Ghost, it was too important. We had to be sure. So, we prayed to God for him to tell us clearly whether they had been filled with the Holy Ghost or not.

God answered us quickly and said yes. We were exceedingly glad and satisfied. But, to our shame and astonishment, God also said that Daniel had been filled with the Holy Ghost before now. God did not tell us when, neither did we know. We suspected it was during one of our weekly Thursday night prayer services or during one of our three daily prayer times. God would later let us know that Daniel had received the Holy Ghost when he was

(3) three years old during one of our weekly night services. Although we were shamed and rightly so, for not knowing our son was already filled with the Holy Ghost, our joy was rekindled and we went immediately and baptized Daniel Isaiah and Rebekah Anna in the name of Jesus for the remission of their sins to complete their born again experience.

REASONS TO WANT TO BE SAVED

Why would you want to be saved?
Well, I will give you three good reasons
to want to be saved. You might say,
I don't need to be saved. You might
say, I'm doing just fine like I am. Well,
you might have an argument if you
could guarantee the future would be
what you want it to be. You might have
an argument if you could guarantee
that you will be living next year. You
might have an argument if you could
guarantee that you will be living next
month. You might have an argument
if you could guarantee that you will
be living next week. You might have
an argument if you could guarantee
that you will be living tomorrow. You
might have an argument if you could
guarantee you will not die today. You
might have an argument if you could
guarantee that you will not die the next
hour. You might have an argument if
you can ensure that you will be living
the next five minutes. If you had
control over your time of life, you might
not need Jesus' salvation. But, since

Jesus, the God Almighty, has control over your appointed time of life, if you are not totally stupid, then you should realize that you need to be saved.

This is the bottom line, either ignorance or stupidity causes you not to get saved. Jesus, the God Almighty, before the world was created, assigned an appointed time for each of us to be born. He, also, set the exact time of our death. Jesus has assigned us our parking meter of life. Who is familiar with a prepaid cell phone? Well, for a prepaid cell phone, you have an allotted amount of minutes to use your cell phone. Once you have used all of your minutes, it is useless. It is dead. Well, Jesus, the God Almighty, has assigned us our prepaid cell phone of life. Do you know how many minutes you have left? Supposed you have (15) fifteen minutes left. Suppose (10) ten. Suppose (5) five. Do you know whether an earthquake will now occur at this place or not? Do you know whether an airplane will now or not crash into this building? Do you know whether a terrorist will now or not blow up this building? Jesus knows.

Do you know whether you will or will not fall dead in this minute of a heart attack? Do you know on the way from here whether you will have an head on collision with another vehicle and be killed? Jesus knows. Your time clock of life is running out!

The number one trick of Satan is to convince those that are not saved, who want to be saved, that you have more time, until your parking meter of life expires. He hopes to convince you that you have more time, until your prepaid cell phone of life is used up.

You might be one of the fools that might say, that you do not care whether you die without being saved. If this is you, you are indeed a fool. One of the main reasons to get saved is to stay out of hell. If you are one of the ones that say you do not care whether you die without being saved, then you probably do not understand that there is a hell with a wide opened mouth waiting to swallow you. Hell is a real place. When death occurs, you, the real you, your soul, will either go to hell or heaven. If you are saved, you go to heaven. If you are not saved, you go to hell. What is hell, you might ask? Hell is a place where souls are tormented with fire. A very, very, very, hot fire. The hottest fire that we can make on earth, spirits can touch it, walk in, lay on, etc., without it burning them. Spirits are beings that include angels and devils. God, also, is a spirit. Hell is so hot that it burns spirits. Not God, but other Spirits. A person's soul is spirit. A person's soul is the person's desire, feeling, emotions, mind, hearing, sight, taste, smell and memory. The real person. The real you. The body dies and rots. The soul is eternal. It will live either in hell or with God, forever and ever more. Hell is a place located in the center of the earth. Those that are in hell are in continual torment. They are burning continually. There is no relief. Just continual screaming and burning. No rest day nor night. There is no water. There is no air conditioner. There is no fan. There is no kind of cooling. Remember, understand, that they have their feelings in hell. Remember, understand, that they have their desires in hell. Their desire to quench their thirst can never be satisfied. Their desire to alter their circumstances can never be done. Their desire to leave hell will never be fulfilled. They will be in their forever. Their cry out to God for help will be in vain. Hopelessness! Hopelessness! Hopelessness! Pain of burning continually. The pain from a burning fire, if not the worst, is one of the worse pains that you can have. Pains on your hands. Pains on your feet. Pains on your arms. Pains on your legs. Pains on your back. Pains on your belly. Pains on your chest. Pains on your face. Pains on your ears. Pains on your tongue. Pains on the top of your head. Pain everywhere. Pains all the time. All day and all night forever and ever and ever and ever and evermore. They had an alternative, they had another choice, they could have gotten saved.

This is the second good reason to want to get saved. For those of you that believe that there is a God, then you should want to be saved for your love to God. You know that God is a good God, the good God. You know that God has been good to you. You cannot live without God. You cannot walk without God. You cannot talk without God. You cannot eat without God. You cannot sleep without God. You cannot love without God. You cannot be loved without God. You cannot breathe without God. All of these things and many, many, other good things God provides you. And, not only you, but all others even his enemies. Even those that curse him. Even those who prefer to serve Satan rather than God himself. It was God who protected you from death. It was Satan who tried to kill you. It was God who healed you. It was Satan that made you sick. It was Satan who killed your love ones. It was God who protected your love ones from Satan that allowed them to live as long as they did.

To get saved is to show your love and gratitude to God. To get saved is to show your love and gratitude to God for a price that he paid for your salvation. The price was very great. God allowed his Son Jesus of Nazareth to die. There have been some men who have allowed their sons to die for what they considered a good cause or for a friend. God allowed his son to die for his enemies. God, even, allowed his Son to suffer for his enemies. To suffer such suffering never suffered before. Unbearable sufferings. God allowed him to be slapped. God allowed him to be spit on. God allowed his beard to be pulled off of his face, causing pain and bleeding and swelling. God allowed a crown made of thorns to be put on his head. Shoved into his scalp and forehead, causing pain, bleeding and swelling. God allowed his Son to be beat with (39) thirty-nine strokes of a whip that would snatch the meat off his bones. Pain, excruciating pain, bleeding and swelling. God allowed him to be nailed on a tree in his hands and feet, causing pain, excruciating pain, bleeding and swelling. God saw his son suffer. He saw his body bleed, from the top of his head to the bottom of his feet. God saw his Son's body swell, from the top of his head to the bottom of his feet. God saw his Son's body from the top of his head to the bottom of his feet change to a painful black and blue-like color with pain and red with blood. He saw him agonize in pain and misery, until through the bleeding and swelling he was not recognizable as a man. We would not and could not allow our sons and daughters, who we loved, to suffer even for a friend, let along their enemies. All that God has done for us, so much, and He only requires for a token of love, for us to accept his glorious salvation. For us to stay out of hell. So, for those who believe that there is a God, God Almighty, then our love for God should make us want to be saved. To get saved is to show that God's sacrifice of His Son was not in vain with us. This salvation of ours makes God's investment yield a return. So great investment for such a little return. Without your salvation the little return is even smaller. Just think, by getting saved, the God that created the universe will allow us to be with him for ever and ever more. It will not be just any existence, but God has promised us in the Holy Bible, that we will have no more sorrow, no more pain, no more crying and no more death. I believe that God has allowed me to experience

how it will be in heaven. Not long after
I was filled with the Holy Ghost, while
living in Montgomery, Alabama, God
gave me a visitation. While sitting in my
bed, with my legs and my feet in the
bed, eyes wide opened, the presence,
the glory, the anointing of God, moved
on me. I felt it. I knew somehow it was
God. I don't know how I knew, but I
knew without a shadow of doubt that
it was God. The sensation, the feeling,
started at the bottom of my feet. It
then covered my feet. It proceeded up
my legs. It continued up my body. It
covered my thighs. It just continued to
go up my body. It covered my belly and
chest. Then it went in my shoulders and
through my arms, hands and fingers.
It went up my neck and covered my
head. It was all over me. Let me try
to tell you how it felt. Words cannot
properly explain how good it felt. This
felt at least a hundred times better
than the best feeling I have ever had.
There is nothing we have experience
to compare with it. Let me tell you
this. Everything on me felt good. My
fingernails, even, felt good. My hair,
even, felt good. Even each strand of

hair felt good. It felt so good until I
started asking God to allow those that
I knew to experience it. I started calling
out their names for God to allow them
to feel it. I mentioned my mother,
brother, sisters, grandmother, nieces,
nephews, aunts, uncles, first cousins,
second cousins, other relatives, friends,
co-workers, college classmates that
were friends, church members and
maybe some others, for God to allow to
experience what I was feeling. I don't
know the exact time, this feeling, this
presence, this anointing, this visitation,
lasted. It was a long time. Maybe an
hour or longer. I believe God allowed
me to experience what heaven feels
like. People, if this is what heaven
feels like, this along is worth getting
saved for.

Now I will address the third good
reason to get saved. If you are one
who thinks that to be saved has no
present life benefit, consider this. Soon
in these days, there will be a great
tormenting plague to cover the whole
earth. This will happen very soon; even
during the time of President Barack

Obama's Presidency. This torment will
be excruciating pain. This pain will be
continual. It will affect all ages, babies,
young children, teenagers, young adults,
middle age adults, senior citizens,
all. The pain of this plague will be so
horrible, until the people will want to
die. People will want to commit suicide.
There will be no medicine for cure.
There will be no medicine for relief.
There will be screaming all over the
earth. The children will be screaming.
The parents will be screaming. The
grandparents will be screaming. The
great grandparents will be screaming.
The nurses will be screaming. The
doctors will be screaming. Those of the
police force will be screaming. Those
of the army will be screaming. Those of
the Air Force will be screaming. Those of
the Navy will be screaming. Those of the
Marines will be screaming. The members
of the House of Representatives will
be screaming. The Senators will be
screaming. The Supreme Court Justices
will be screaming. The Vice President
will be screaming. The President will be
screaming. The Pope will scream. All will
scream!

All of this paining. All of this misery. All of this hurting and no relief. No relief for five months. Yes! It will last for (5) five months. And think about this. It is hard to get sleep when you are in pain. What hopelessness. The curse of this plague will be so bad that people will want to die. However, the curse of this plague will not allow them to die. This curse has been told about in the Book of Revelation of the Holy Bible. Turn to the Book of Revelation in your Bible. Look at Chapter (9) Nine. Read Verse (6) Six.

Revelation Ch.9, V.6
"And in those days shall men seek death, and shall not find it; and shall desire to die and death shall flee from them."

This great excruciating painful plague will soon happen. This painful plague will be the closest thing to hell itself. It will be so horrible, so excruciating, that God told me to write a book about it to warn the people. This is the book here. The name is "Five Month Desire To Die, But Not Possible When Fifth Angel

Blows Trumpet." The only ones on planet Earth that will not be affected with this great painful plague, will be those that have the Holy Ghost. You must have the Holy Ghost to be saved. All that have the Holy Ghost speak in tongues.

If you, yet, after reading this, due to some custom, tradition or religion, do not get saved, it is because you are too stupid to get saved.

THE FOUR EASY STEPS TO GET SAVED/ BORN AGAIN:

1. Repent:
    a. ask God to forgive your sins, ask in the name of Jesus;
    b. surrender your will for God's will to be done in your life.
2. Ask God to save you, to fill you with the Holy Ghost, ask in the name of Jesus.
3. Do not ask God anymore to save you, just thank God, praise God for saving you. You must thank

God in the name of Jesus. At the point of your greatest sincerity, you will speak in another language. This will be your sign of confirmation. God will be using your mouth to speak a language spoken somewhere on earth that you have not learned. This is your sign that you are born of the Spirit.

4. Get baptized in the name of Jesus Christ.

John Ch.3,Vs.3&5

"Jesus answered...Except a man be born again, he cannot see the kingdom of God...Jesus answered... Except a man be born of water and of the Spirit he cannot enter into the kingdom of God."

John Ch.3,V.8

"...thou hearest the sound thereof...so is everyone that is born of the Spirit."

Colossians Ch.3,V.17

"And whatsoever ye do in word or deed, do all in the name of the Lord Jesus..."

LIST OF BOOKS THAT WE HAVE WRITTEN:

1. Proof That **YOUR LEADERS** Have **DECEIVED YOU** And The End Times

2. What **GOD** Is Now Telling His Prophets **ABOUT** The **END TIMES**

3. Five Month **DESIRE TO DIE**, But Not Possible When Fifth Angel Blows Trumpet

4. **GOD's** Word Concerning **MARRIAGE AND DIVORCE**

5. The Name Of The (Anti-Christ) Beast And **666** Identification

6. **WHERE GOD's PEOPLE** (Saints) **GO** When GOD Comes Back To Get Us

7. How You Can **PROVE** That **YOU HAVE** A **SOUL**

8. **JESUS** Was **NOT CRUCIFIED WHEN** As Has Been **TAUGHT**

18. The **NAME OF** The **(ANTI-CHRIST) BEAST**

19. **WHO IS** The **(FALSE PROPHET)** Second Beast

20. **WHY, WHEN** And **HOW** The (Anti-Christ) Beast **WILL DECEIVE** The World That **HE IS GOD**

21. The **TEN HORNS** Of The Books Of **DANIEL** And **REVELATION**

22. **UNDERSTANDING** The **BOOK OF** Revelation To Understand the Book Of **REVELATION**

23. Main Arguments For The **RAPTURE** Being **BEFORE** The **GREAT TRIBULATION** And Why They Are **NOT TRUE**

24. **MAKING SATAN** And His Kingdom **PAY** A Big Price **SO** The **END CAN COME**

25. Makeup, Membership And Money Of **GOD'S CHURCH** And **HOW GOD WANTS** Them To Be

Before & During The Great Tribulation")

HOW TO GET SAVED

To Be Saved You must Speak with
Tongues & Be Baptized in the Name
of Jesus

John Ch. 3, V. 3
"Jesus answered... Except a man be
born again, he cannot see the Kingdom
of God."

John Ch. 3, V. 5
"Jesus answered... Except a man be
born of water and of the Spirit, he
cannot enter into the Kingdom of God."

Acts Ch. 2, V. 38
"... Repent, and be baptized every
one of you in the name of Jesus Christ
for the remission of sins, and ye shall
receive the gift of the Holy Ghost."

How to Repent: (1) Sincerely ask God
to forgive your sins, ask in the name of
Jesus; (2) Surrender your will for God's
Will to be done in your life.

<u>After Repenting</u>: Sincerely ask God to save you, to give you his Spirit, to give you the Holy Ghost, to have you to speak with other tongues. [Once you have asked, then just continue to thank God for doing so, just praise him, sincerely. You WILL then speak in tongues.]

<u>John Ch. 3, V. 8</u>
"… thou hearest the sound thereof…so is everyone that is born of the Spirit."

<u>After Speaking in Tongues</u>: Get baptized in the name of Jesus, again you must be repented.
<u>NOTE</u>: You can be baptized and then receive the Holy Ghost or be filled with the Holy Ghost then be baptized.

<u>Speaking in Tongues</u>: Speaking in tongues (unknown language) is God speaking through you.

<u>Mark Ch. 16, V. 17</u>
"And these signs shall follow them that believe… they shall speak with new tongues."

Acts Ch. 2, V. 4
"... and began to speak with other tongues as the Spirit gave them utterance."

Acts Ch. 22, V 16
"... be baptized, and wash away thy sins..."

Colossians Ch. 3, V. 17
"And whatsoever ye do in word or deed, do all in the name of the Lord Jesus..."

The name of the Father is Jesus, the name of the Son is Jesus, the name of the Holy Ghost is Jesus.

John Ch. 17, V. 26
"And I have declared thy name unto them..."

John Ch. 5, V. 43 "
"I am come in my Father's name..."

Hebrews Ch. 1, V. 4
"... he hath by inheritance obtained a more excellent name..."

<u>John Ch. 4, V. 24</u>
"God is a Spirit..."

<u>Question</u>: Is the Father Holy? Answer: Yes. God is a Father; God was manifested in flesh as a Son; God is a Spirit, the Holy Spirit, the Holy Ghost.

I, Frederick E. Franklin, am a Father, am a Son, am a Human Being. Father, Son, Holy Ghost and Father, Son, Human Being are titles. God's name is Jesus.

<u>Matthew Ch. 28, V. 19</u>
"... Teach all nations, baptizing them in the name of ... the Son..."

TO BE A PART OF THE F&SF MINISTRY FOR JESUS THE FOLLOWING WILL BE EXPECTED:

II Timothy Ch.2, V.3
"Thou therefore endure hardness, as a good soldier of Jesus Christ."

Ephesians Ch.6, V.10
"... be strong in the Lord, and in the power of his might."

Ephesians Ch.5, V.27
"That he might present it to himself a glorious church, not having spot, or wrinkle, or any such thing; but that it should be holy and without blemish."

The F&SF Ministry For JESUS Soldier Will:

1.   Be Filled With The Holy Ghost (Evidenced By Speaking In Tongues)

2.   Be Baptized In The Name Of JESUS

3.   Be Honest And Sincere

4. Have Love And Compassion For Others

5. Properly Pay Tithes And Give Offerings

6. Believe In One God (The God Of Abraham, Isaac, And Jacob)

7. Worship Only God Almighty, The Creator Of The Universe, JESUS

8. Be Holy

9. Attend Sabbath (Friday Dark To Saturday Dark) Service(s)

10. Attend Other Service(s) When Possible

11. Make Continuous Sincere Efforts For Souls To Be Saved

12. Profess/Testify That You Must Speak In Tongues And Be Baptized In The Name Of Jesus To Be Saved

13. Profess/Testify That The Great Tribulation Is Before The Rapture

14. Reveal That Pope John Paul II Is The (Anti-Christ) Beast

15. Be Bold (Not A Coward)

16. Desire To Grow In Revelation And Power Of God

17. Be Faithful And Dedicated To The F&SF Ministry For JESUS

18. Receive/Accept The Teachings Of Apostle Frederick E. Franklin

19. Not Espouse Teachings/Doctrines Contrary To That Of Apostle Frederick E. Franklin

20. Adhere To The Leadership Of Apostle Frederick E. Franklin

21. Not Be A Liar

22. Not Be A Hypocrite

23. Not Be A Witchcraft Worker

24. Not Be A Partaker Of Idolatry.

EXCERPTS FROM OUR BOOK "THE NAME OF THE (ANTI-CHRIST) BEAST AND 666 IDENTIFICATION"

There will be great deception. The scriptures indicate that the (Anti-Christ) Beast, Pope John Paul II, Carol Josef Wojtyla, will fake his death. Later on, to fake being resurrected from the dead. All to the end, to fake that he is God. All to the end, to discredit JESUS' resurrection. All to the end, to discredit that JESUS is God and rather to show/deceive that he is God.

<u>Revelation Ch. 17, V. 8</u>
"...the beast that was, and is not, and yet is."

The Above scripture indicates that the Beast, Pope John Paul II, Carol Josef Wojtyla, was living. It further indicates that he will seem not to be living, but he actually will be living. He was living. He appears not to be living. But, he yet is living.

WHERE TO PURCHASE OUR BOOKS

BY FREDERICK E. FRANKLIN

BOOKSTORE SALES:
(25,000 BOOKSTORES)

1. BARNES & NOBLE
2. BOOKS A MILLION
3. ETC.

INTERNET SALES:
AMAZON . COM

DIRECT SALES:
2669 MEADOWVIEW DR.
MOBILE, ALABAMA 36695
PH. # : (251) 644-4329

JESUS IS GOD

1. <u>I John Chapter 5, Verse 20</u>
"And we know that the Son of
God is come, and hath given us an
understanding, that we may know him
that is true, and we are in him that is
true, even in his Son Jesus Christ. This is
the true God, and eternal life."

2. <u>John Chapter 1, Verses 1 & 14</u>
"In the beginning was the Word, and
the Word was with God, and the Word
was God. And the Word was made
flesh, and dwelt among us, (and we
beheld his glory, the glory as of the only
begotten of the Father,) full of grace
and truth."

3. <u>I Timothy Chapter 3, Verse 16</u>
"And without controversy great is the
mystery of godliness: God was manifest
in the flesh, justified in the Spirit, seen
of angels, preached unto the Gentiles,
believed on in the world, received up
into glory."

4. Isaiah Chapter 9, Verse 6
"For unto us a child is born, unto us a son is given: and the government shall be upon his shoulder: and his name shall be called Wonderful, Counsellor, The mighty God, The everlasting Father, The Prince of Peace."

5. Matthew Chapter 1, Verse 23
"Behold, a virgin shall be with child, and shall bring forth a son, and they shall call his name Emmanuel, which being interpreted is, God with us."

6. Titus Chapter 1, Verses 3 & 4
"...God our Saviour;...the Lord Jesus Christ our Saviour."

7. Isaiah Chapter 43, Verse 11
"I, even I, am the Lord; and beside me there is no Saviour."

8. Isaiah Chapter 44, Verse 6
"Thus saith the Lord the King of Israel, and his redeemer the Lord of hosts; I am the first, and I am the last; and beside me there is no God."

9. <u>Revelation Chapter 1, Verses 17 & 18</u>
"...I am the first and the last: I am he that liveth, and was dead..."

10. <u>Revelation Chapter 22, Verses 13 & 16</u>
"I am Alpha and Omega, the beginning and the end, the first and the last. I Jesus have sent mine angel to testify unto you these things in the churches..."

11. <u>Isaiah Chapter 44, Verse 24</u>
"Thus saith the Lord, thy redeemer, and he that formed thee from the womb, I am the Lord that maketh all things; that stretcheth forth the heavens alone; that spreadeth abroad the earth by myself..."

12. <u>Colossians Chapter 1, Verses 16, 17 & 18</u>
"For by him were all things created, that are in heaven, and that are in earth, visible and invisible, whether they be thrones, or powers: all things were created by him, and for him: And he is before all things, and by him all

things consist. And he is the head of the body the church."

13. <u>Ephesians Chapter 5, Verse 23</u>
"For the husband is the head of the wife, even as Christ is the head of the church: and he is the saviour of the body."

14. <u>Colossians Chapter 2, Verse 9</u>
"For in Him dwelleth all the fullness of the Godhead bodily."

15. <u>I John Chapter 5, Verse 7</u>
"...three that bear record in heaven, the Father, the Word, and the Holy Ghost: and these three are one."

16. <u>Revelation Chapter 15, Verse 3</u>
"...Great and Marvelous are thy works, Lord God Almighty; just and true are thy ways, thou King of saints."

17. <u>Revelation Chapter 17, Verse 14</u>
"...and the Lamb shall overcome them: for he is Lord of lords, and King of kings; and they that are with him are called, and chosen, and faithful."

18. <u>I Thessalonians Chapter 3, Verse 13</u>
"...God, even our Father, at the coming of our Lord Jesus Christ with all his saints."

19. <u>Zechariah Chapter 14, Verse 5</u>
"...and the Lord my God shall come, and all the saints with thee."

20. <u>I John Chapter 3, Verse 16</u>
"Hereby perceive we the love of God, because he laid down his life for us."

21. Etc.

<u>THE FOUR EASY STEPS TO GET SAVED/ BORN AGAIN</u>:

1.　Repent:
　　a. ask God to forgive your sins, ask in the name of Jesus;
　　b. surrender your will for God's will to be done in your life.
2.　Ask God to save you, to fill you with the Holy Ghost, ask in the name of Jesus.
3.　Do not ask God anymore to save you, just thank God, praise God for saving you. You must thank

God in the name of Jesus. At the point of your greatest sincerity, you will speak in another language. This will be your sign of confirmation. God will be using your mouth to speak a language spoken somewhere on earth that you have not learned. This is your sign that you are born of the Spirit.

4. Get baptized in the name of Jesus Christ.

John Ch.3,Vs.3&5
"Jesus answered...Except a man be born again, he cannot see the kingdom of God...Jesus answered... Except a man be born of water and of the Spirit he cannot enter into the kingdom of God."

John Ch.3,V.8
"...thou hearest the sound thereof...so is everyone that is born of the Spirit."

Colossians Ch.3,V.17
"And whatsoever ye do in word or deed, do all in the name of the Lord Jesus..."

THE SABBATH

What Is The Sabbath?
The Sabbath is a holy day ordained by God to be so. It is a day for all to cease from work.

When Is The Sabbath?
The Sabbath is the last day, the seventh day of the week.

Genesis Ch.2, Vs. 1-3
"Thus the heavens and earth were finished, and all of the host of them. And on the seventh day God ended his work which he had made; and he rested on the seventh day from all his work which he had made."

Exodus Ch.20, Vs. 8-11
"Remember the sabbath day, to keep it holy. Six days shalt thou labour, and do all thy work: But the seventh day is the sabbath of the Lord thy God: in it thou shalt not do any work, thou, nor thy son, nor thy daughter, thy manservant, nor thy cattle, nor thy stranger that is within thy gates: For in six days the Lord

made heaven and earth, the sea, and all
that in them is, and rested the seventh
day: wherefore the Lord blessed the
sabbath day, and hallowed it."

Exodus Ch.23, V. 12
"Six days thou shalt do thy work, and
on the seventh day thou shalt rest: that
thine ox and thine ass may rest, and the
son of thy handmaid, and the stranger,
may be refreshed."

When Does The Day Start?
The day starts at dark and goes to the
next day at dark.

Genesis Ch.1, Vs 5, 8, 13, 19, 23 & 31
"…And the evening and the morning
were the first day…And the evening
and the morning were the second day.
And the evening and the morning were
the third day. And the evening and the
morning were the fourth day. And the
evening and the morning were the
fifth day. And God saw every thing that
he had made and, behold, it was very
good. And the evening and the morning
were the sixth day."

Is It A Sin To NOT Keep Or Violate The Sabbath?

To keep the Sabbath is one of the ten commandments. One of the ten commandments say thou shalt not kill. Another says thou shalt not steal. Just as it is sin to kill and steal, likewise, is it a sin to NOT keep or to violate the Sabbath.

Exodus Ch.20, V. 13-15
"Thou shalt not kill. Thou shalt not commit adultery. Thou shalt not steal."

What You Should Not Do On The Sabbath.

Exodus Ch.20, V. 10
"But the seventh day is the sabbath of the Lord thy God: in it thou shalt not do any work, thou, nor thy son, nor thy daughter, thy manservant, nor thy maidservant, nor thy cattle, nor thy stranger that is within thy gates..."

Nehemiah Ch.10, V. 31
"And if the people of the land bring ware or any victuals on the sabbath day to sell, that we would not buy it

of them on the sabbath, or on the
holy day..."

Nehemiah Ch.13, Vs. 16-18
"There dwelt men of Tyre also therein,
which brought fish, and all manner of
ware, and sold on the sabbath unto the
children of Judah, and in Jerusalem.
Then I contended with nobles of Judah,
and said unto them, What evil thing
is this that ye do, and profane the
sabbath day? Did not your fathers thus,
and did not our God bring all this wrath
upon this city? Yet ye bring more wrath
upon Israel by profaning the sabbath."

What Happened When The Sabbath Was Not Kept Or Violated Intentionally.
Numbers Ch.15, Vs. 32-36
"And while the children of Israel were
in the wilderness, they found a man
that gathered sticks upon the sabbath
day. And they that found him gathering
sticks brought him unto Moses and
Aaron and unto all the congregation.
And they put him in ward, because
it was not declared what should be
done unto him. And the Lord said unto

Moses, The man shall be surely put to death: all the congregation shall stone him with stones without the camp. And all the congregation brought him without the camp, and stone with stones and he died; as the Lord commanded Moses."

Numbers Ch.15, Vs. 30-31
"But the soul that doeth ought presumptuously, whether he be born in the land, or a stranger, the same reproacheth the Lord; and that soul shall be cut off from among his people. Because he hath despised the word of the Lord, and hath broken his commandment, that soul shall be utterly cut off; his iniquity shall be upon him."

Not Keeping Or Violating The Sabbath Out Of Ignorance.
Numbers Ch.15, Vs. 27-28
"And if any soul sin through ignorance... the priest shall make atonement for the soul that sinneth ignorantly, when he sinneth by ignorance before the Lord, to make atonement for him; and it shall be forgiven him."

<u>Numbers Ch.15, Vs. 22, 24 & 25</u>
"And if ye erred, and not observed at all
these commandments...Then if it shall
be, if ought be committed by ignorance
without the knowledge...the priest
shall make an atonement for all the
congregation of the children of Israel,
and it shall be forgiven them..."

Other Benefits Of Keeping The Sabbath.
God is pleased with those who obey
his word and the promises of the Holy
Bible is available to you.

<u>Isaiah Ch.56, Vs. 2 & 5-7</u>
"Blessed is the man that doeth this,
and the son of man that layeth hold
on it; that keepeth the sabbath from
polluting it, and keep his hand from
doing any evil. Even unto them will I
give in mine house and within my walls
a place and a name better than the
sons and daughters. I will give them
an everlasting name, that shall not be
cut off. Also the sons of the stranger
that join themselves to the Lord, to
serve him, and to love the name of the
Lord, to be his servants, every one that
keepeth the sabbath from polluting

it, and taketh hold of my covenant;
Even them will I bring unto my holy
mountain, and make them joyful in
my house of prayer...their sacrifices
shall be accepted upon mine altar; for
mine house shall be called an house of
prayer for all people."

Exodus Ch.23, V. 12
"...thou shalt rest...be refreshed."

Exodus Ch.20, V.12
"...the Lord blessed the sabbath day,
and hallowed it."

Why Has Sunday Been Chosen As The So-Called Sabbath By The So-Called Christians And Some Christians?

The Pope of 325 A.D. birth this
blasphemy of changing the Sabbath
day from the seventh day to the first
day of the week. This blasphemous
change of the sabbath to Sunday was
done to have the people worship
God the Almighty on the same day as
the worship of the sun god. Sunday
the worship of the Sun god. This
blasphemous change was prophesied of
in the scriptures.

Matthew Ch.24, V. 24

"For there shall arise false Christs, and false prophets, and shall shew great signs and wonders; insomuch that, if it were possible, they shall deceive the very elect."

Daniel Ch.7, V. 25

"And he shall speak great words against the most High, and shall wear out the saints of the most High, and think to change times and laws…"

Daniel Ch.8, V. 12

"An host was given him against the daily sacrifice by reason of transgression, and it cast down the truth to the ground; and it practiced and prospered."

To justify this blasphemous change, he, the Pope, had to use scriptures of the Holy Bible. He used three places in the scriptures.

Matthew Ch.28, Vs. 1-6

"In the end of the sabbath, as it began to dawn toward the first day of the week, came Mary Magdalene and the other Mary to see the sepulchre. And, behold, there was a great earthquake: for the angel of Lord descended from heaven, and came and rolled back the stone from the door, and sat upon it. His countenance was like lightning, and his raiment white as snow; And for fear of him the keepers did shake, and became as dead men. And the angel answered and said unto the women, Fear ye not: for I know that ye seek Jesus, which was crucified. He is not here: for he is risen, as he said. Come, see the place where the Lord lay."

Supposedly, because Jesus was resurrected on the first day of the week, the sabbath should be changed to the first day of the week.

<u>I Corinthians Ch.16, Vs. 1-3</u>
"Now concerning the collection for the saints, as I have given order to the churches of Galatia, even so do ye. Upon the first day of the week let every one of you lay by him in store, as God hath prospered him, that there be no gatherings when I come. And when I come, whosoever ye shall approve by

your letters, them will I send to bring your liberality to Jerusalem."

Supposedly, because Paul told them to take up a collection on the first day of the week, this, therefore, means that the New Testament Church's sabbath is on the first day of the week.

<u>Acts Ch.20, V. 7</u>
"And upon the first day of the week, when the disciples came together to break bread, Paul preached to them, ready to depart on the morrow, and continued his speech until midnight."

Supposedly, because the disciples came together on the first day means that they came to hear the word, and because Paul preached on the first day, supposedly, this shows that the New Testament Church had as its sabbath the first day of the week.

What ridiculous justification(s) to change the Sabbath to the first day of the week.

Scriptures Of The New Testament Refuting The So-Called Sunday Sabbath.

Let us first look at the Pope's last so-called justification, Acts Ch.20, V. 7. When the scriptures said that they came "together to break bread," it means that they came together to eat. While they were there together, Paul took this opportunity to preached to them. Like any preacher would do. Refer to the immediate following scriptures, Acts Ch.20, Vs. 8-12.

Acts Ch.20, Vs. 8-12

"And there were many lights in the upper chamber, where they were gathered together. And there sat in the window a certain young man named Eutychus, being fallen into a deep sleep: and as Paul was long preaching, he sunk down with sleep, and fell down from the third loft, and was taken up dead. And Paul went down, and fell on him, and embracing him said, Trouble not yourselves; for his life is in him. When he therefore was come up again, and had broken bread, and eaten, and talked a long while, even till break of day, so he departed. And they brought the young man alive, and were not a little comforted."

Let us now look at the Pope's I Corinthians Ch.16, Vs. 1-3, justification. Here Paul tells the Church of Corinth to give an offering to the Church in Jerusalem. He said take up collection on the first day of the week. Note that Paul said that there should not be any gathering. The people could not gather on the sabbath day to sell or give their goods or livestock to get a collection, so Paul said do it on the first day of the week. And whatever they gathered on the first day of the week, that is where their offering would come from.

Let us now look at the Pope's third and remaining justification, Matthew Ch.28, Vs. 1-6. These scriptures speak of Jesus' resurrection on the first day of they week. Somehow, this gives us the right to change God's word of a seventh day Sabbath. This is nonsense. God says that there is nothing above his word, not even the name of Jesus.

<u>Psalm 138, V. 2</u>
"I will worship toward thy holy
temple, and praise thy name for thy
lovingkindness and for thy truth: for
thou hast magnified thy word above all
thy name."

Now let us see when Paul, Jews and the
Gentiles, the New Testament Church,
really worshipped. When their Sabbath
actually was.

<u>Acts Ch.18, V. 4</u>
"And he reasoned in the synagogue
every Sabbath, and persuaded the Jews
and the Greeks"

<u>Acts Ch.13, Vs. 13-17, 22-23 & 42-44</u>
"Now when Paul and his company
loosed from Paphos...they came to
Antioch...and went into the synagogue
on the sabbath day, and sat down. And
after the reading of the law and the
prophets the rulers of the synagogue
sent unto them, saying, Ye men and
brethren, if ye have any word of
exhortation for the people, say on.
Then Paul stood up, and beckoning with
his hand said, Men of Israel, and ye that

fear God, give audience. The God of this people of Israel chose our fathers... he raised up unto them David to be their King...Of this man's seed hath God according to his promise raised unto Israel a Savior, Jesus...And when the Jews were gone out of the synagogue, the Gentiles besought that these words might be preached to them the next sabbath. Now when the congregation was broken up, many of the Jews and religious proselytes followed Paul...And the next sabbath day came almost the whole city together to hear the word of God."

Note: Jews that worshipped God, only worshipped on the seventh day, the real Sabbath day.

I Peter Ch.3, Vs. 15-16
"But sanctify the Lord God in your hearts: and be ready always to give an answer to every man that asketh you a reason of the hope that is in you with meekness and fear: Having a good conscience; that, whereas they speak evil of you, as of evildoers, they may be

ashamed that falsely accuse your good conversation in Christ."

What About Colossians Chapter 2, Verse 16?

Colossians Ch.2, V. 16

Let no man judge you in meat, or in drink, or respect of an holyday, or of the new moon, or of the sabbaths..."

There are more than one kind of sabbath referred to in the Holy Bible. There is the seventh day sabbath as has been discussed thus far and there are other sabbaths and holydays. These other sabbaths and holydays are what is referred to in Colossians Chapter 2, Verse 16. These sabbaths included the Passover, feast days, and some other holydays observed by the Jews. Among these days was The Dedication Of The Temple built by Solomon.

John Ch.10, Vs. 22-23

"And it was at Jerusalem the feast of the dedication, and it was winter. And Jesus walked in the temple in Solomon's porch."

Another such sabbath day is referred to in John Chapter 19, Verse 31.

<u>John Ch.19, V. 31</u>
"The Jews therefore, because it was the preparation, that the bodies should not remain upon the cross on the sabbath day, (for that sabbath was an high day,)..."

The lack of understanding of the above scripture is how the Pope of 325 A.D. has been able to deceive the people in celebrating the worship of the Spring goddess. This is the Easter celebration. Refer to our book, "Jesus Was Not Crucified When As Has Been Taught."

Here are some of the scriptures referring to the other sabbaths: Leviticus Ch.19, Vs. 1-3; Leviticus Ch.19, V. 30; Leviticus Ch.16, Vs. 29-31; Leviticus Ch.25, Vs. 1-5; Leviticus Ch.26, Vs. 27-35; Leviticus Ch.23, Vs. 4-7; Leviticus Ch.23, Vs. 15, 21, 23-28, 32-36 & 38-39; I Kings Ch.8, Vs. 63-66; etc.

These are the ordinances that Jesus blotted out, even nailing to them the cross.

SPECIAL EXCEPTIONS TO WORKING ON THE SABBATH:

People who try to get around the word of God concerning not working on the Sabbath, try to use certain instances when JESUS said it was alright to do certain things on the Sabbath. They point to the scriptures when JESUS' disciples were hungry and they plucked corn on the Sabbath. They, also, refer to the scriptures when JESUS healed on the Sabbath; the Pharisees complained that JESUS was working on the Sabbath.

EXPLANATION:

JESUS indicates his justification for the efforts on the Sabbath by two short statements.

1. In The Plucking Of Corn On The Sabbath—

    JESUS says—

    ("The sabbath was made for man, and not man for the sabbath.")

    JESUS does not want or require anyone to starve because it is the Sabbath. Refer to Mark Ch. 2, Vs. 23-28.

<u>Mark Ch. 2, Vs. 23-25&27</u>

"And it came to pass, that he went through the corn fields on the sabbath day: and his disciples began, as they went, to pluck the ears of corn. And the Pharisees said unto him, Behold, why do they on the sabbath day that which is unlawful? And he said unto them, Have ye never read what David did, when he had need, and was a hungred, he, and they that were with him? How he went into the house of God in the days of Abiathar the high priest, and did eat showbread, which is not lawful to eat but for the priest, and gave also to them which were with him? And he said unto them, The sabbath was made for man, and not man for the sabbath.

2. In The Healing On The Sabbath—

JESUS Indicates—

(It is right to do good on the sabbath.)

During the work of God is always permitted, even on the Sabbath. Refer to Luke Ch. 13, Vs. 14,15&16.

<u>Luke Ch. 13, Vs. 14,15&16</u>

"And the ruler of the synagogue answer with indignation, because that Jesus had healed on the Sabbath day, and said unto the people, There are six days in which men ought to work: in them therefore come and be healed, and not sabbath day. The Lord then answered him, and said, Thou hypocrite, doth not each one of you on the sabbath loose his ox or his ass from the stall, and lead him away to watering? And ought not this woman, being a daughter of Abraham, whom Satan hath bound, lo these eighteen years, be loosed from this bond on the sabbath day?"

If there is an emergency or critical need that happens the day of the Sabbath, JESUS does not expect you to ignore it. JESUS does not expect you to let someone suffer or die because it is the Sabbath. This does not include other regularly scheduled jobs or occupations on the Sabbath to meet your family needs. Ministering is always permitted, even on the Sabbath. Except for the above, the work that is not permitted on the Sabbath is work that you do on the six other days of the week.

THE FOUR EASY STEPS TO GET SAVED/ BORN AGAIN:

1.   Repent:
     a. ask God to forgive your sins, ask in the name of Jesus;
     b. surrender your will for God's will to be done in your life.

2.   Ask God to save you, to fill you with the Holy Ghost, ask in the name of Jesus.

3.   Do not ask God anymore to save you, just thank God, praise God for saving you. You must thank God in the name of Jesus. At the point of your greatest sincerity, you will speak in another language. This will be your sign of confirmation. God will be using your mouth to speak a language spoken somewhere on earth that you have not learned. This is your sign that you are born of the Spirit.

4.   Get baptized in the name of Jesus Christ.

John Ch.3,Vs.3&5

"Jesus answered...Except a man be born again, he cannot see the kingdom of God...Jesus answered... Except a man be born of water and of the Spirit he cannot enter into the kingdom of God."

John Ch.3,V.8

"...thou hearest the sound thereof...so is everyone that is born of the Spirit."

Colossians Ch.3,V.17

"And whatsoever ye do in word or deed, do all in the name of the Lord Jesus…"

CONTACT PAGE

We provide this page for those of you who desire to get in contact with us regarding:

I.   Ministering
       A. Preaching
       B. Singing
       C. Being prayed for

II.   Ordering tapes
       A. Audio of this book
       B. Preaching
       C. Singing
       D. Additional end times
          prophecies

III.   Ordering books

IV.   Questions concerning our
       next book

V.   Other questions.

Remember to give your address. For a quicker response, provide a telephone number where you can be reached.

Frederick & Sylvia Franklin's
Ministry for JESUS
2669 Meadowview Drive
Mobile, AL, 36695
Telephone #: (251) 644-4329

About The Author

"What Was Cain's Mark?" was written by Apostle Frederick E. Franklin of the ministry of F & SF Ministry For JESUS. What has been written is revelation from God that has been given to Frederick and his wife Sylvia. Frederick E. Franklin is an apostle, prophet and end times preacher. His wife, Sylvia Franklin, is a prophetess, evangelist and singer. The ministry positions stated above are what God, himself, has said/ordained and anointed them to be. Frederick and Sylvia have three children, Elijah Jeremiah Ezekiel Franklin, Daniel Isaiah Franklin, and Rebekah Anna Franklin. Frederick E. Franklin was a successful electrical engineer in private industry, state and federal government and also self-employment, before he was born again and told by God to preach.

TO THE SAINTS AND THOSE WHO HAVE RECEIVED THE WORDS OF THIS BOOK

I Say Unto The Saints Be Blessed! I Speak Blessings To You! I Rebuke The Bondages Out Of Your Lives! I Destroy The Delay & Hindrances To Your Prayers Being Answered! I Speak Deliverance To Your Body & Your Mind! I Rebuke The Lies Of Satan From Your Thinking! I Speak Blessings Of Money & Finances To You! I Decree The Wealth Of The Sinner To Come Unto You! I Speak Devine & Perfect Health To You! I Destroy The Yokes & Bondages That Prevent You From Having Household Salvation! I Decree & Speak These Blessings In The Name Of My Lord JESUS Christ, The Saviour & Healer & Deliverer & Provider & Miracle Worker!

To The Saints & Others Who Have Received The Words Of This Book, Some Of You Have Been Healed & Delivered & Some Of You Have Been Filled With The Holy Ghost, From The Reading Or Hearing The Words Of This Book. We Have Ministered To You In Revelation. I Will Now Minister To You In Power As An Apostle Of God, In The Name Of My Lord JESUS Christ:

For The Sick, Afflicted & Diseased Be Healed, Be Made Whole, In The Name Of My Lord JESUS Christ, The Saviour & Healer & Miracle Worker!

I Curse The Curse That Have Put You In Bondage, In The Name Of My Lord JESUS Christ, The Saviour & Healer & Deliverer & Miracle Worker!

Whether It Be A Mental Or Physical Curse, I Rebuke It, In The Name Of My Lord JESUS Christ, The Saviour & Healer & Deliverer & Miracle Worker!

I Curse Blindness, In The Name Of My Lord JESUS Christ, The Saviour & Healer & Miracle Worker!

I Curse Deafness, In The Name Of My Lord JESUS Christ, The Saviour & Healer & Miracle Worker!

I Curse & Rebuke Every Dumb Spirit From You, In The Name Of y Lord JESUS Christ, The Saviour & Healer & Deliverer & Miracle Worker!

I Curse Lameness & Every Paralyzed Condition From You, In The Of My Lord JESUS Christ, The Saviour & Healer & Miracle Worker!

I Cast Out Every Mental Retardation Spirit, In The Name Of My Lord JESUS, The Saviour & Healer & Deliverer & Miracle Worker!

I Curse Cancer & Every Tumor From The Top Of Your Head To The Bottom Of Your Feet, In The Name Of My Lord JESUS Christ, The Saviour & Healer & Miracle Worker!

I Curse Arthritis, Bursitis, Tendonitis & Gout, In The Name Of My Lord JESUS Christ, The Saviour & Healer & Miracle Worker!

I Rebuke & Curse Pain, Throbbing, Toothache & Shingles, In The Name Of My Lord JESUS Christ, The Saviour & Healer & Deliverer & Miracle Worker!

I Rebuke & Curse Infections & Sores, In The Name Of My Lord JESUS Christ, The Saviour & Healer & Miracle Worker!

I Rebuke Every Spirit Of Depression, In The Name Of My Lord JESUS Christ, The Saviour & Healer & Deliverer & Miracle Worker!

I Curse & Rebuke Every Devil Of Down Syndrome, Arthritis & Schizophrenia, In The Name Of My Lord JESUS Christ, The Saviour & Healer & Deliverer & Miracle Worker!

I Rebuke & Curse Every Addiction To Alcohol, Nicotine, Cocaine, Meth & Other Dope, In The Name Of My Lord JESUS Christ, The Saviour & Deliverer & Miracle Worker!

I Speak Healing & Deliverance To You Of Migraines & Other Headaches, In The Name Of My Lord JESUS Christ, The Saviour & Healer & Deliverer & Miracle Worker!

I Command Every Blood Clout, Obstruction & Hindrance To Blood Flow To Be Dissolved, In The Name Of My Lord JESUS Christ, The Saviour & Healer & Miracle Worker!

I Speak Healing In Your Blood, In The Name Of My Lord JESUS Christ, The Saviour & Healer & Miracle Worker!

I Speak Healing In Your Nerves, In The Name Of My Lord JESUS Christ, The Saviour & Healer & Miracle Worker!

I Speak Healing To Your Back, In The Name Of My Lord JESUS Christ, The Saviour & Healer & Miracle Worker!

I Rebuke Every Deformity, In The Name Of My Lord JESUS Christ, The Saviour & Healer & Miracle Worker!

Be Healed In Your Bowels, In The Name Of
My Lord JESUS Christ, The Saviour & Healer &
Miracle Worker!

I Rebuke High Blood Pressure, In The Name Of
My Lord JESUS Christ, The Saviour & Healer &
Miracle Worker!

I Curse Diabetes, In The Name Of My Lord
JESUS Christ, The Saviour & Healer & Miracle
Worker!

I Curse Kidney Problems, In The Name Of My
Lord JESUS Christ, The Saviour & Healer &
Miracle Worker!

I Speak Healing To Your Bladder, In The Name
Of My Lord JESUS Christ, The Saviour & Healer
& Miracle Worker!

I Curse Excess Fat & Obesity, I Speak & Decree
A Creative Miracle To You, In The Name Of
My Lord JESUS Christ, The Saviour & Healer &
Deliverer & Miracle Worker!

I Speak & Decree A Reconstruction Creative
Miracle To Your Ear(s), Noise, Eye(s), Jaw &
Chin, In The Name Of My Lord JESUS Christ,
The Saviour & Healer & Miracle Worker!

I Speak & Decree A Creative Miracle To Your Spine, In The Name Of My Lord JESUS Christ, The Saviour & Healer & Miracle Worker!

I Rebuke Scoliosis & Speak & Decree A Creative Miracle To Your Spine, In The Name Of My Lord JESUS Christ, The Saviour & Healer & Miracle Worker!

I Curse Gall Stones & Kidney Stones, I Command You Dissolve & Disappear, In The Name Of My Lord JESUS Christ, The Saviour & Healer & Miracle Worker!

I Speak Healing To Your Heart, In The Name Of My Lord JESUS Christ, The Saviour & Healer & Miracle Worker!

I Speak Healing In Your Lungs & Breathing, In The Name Of My Lord JESUS Christ, The Saviour & Healer & Miracle Worker!

I Rebuke Feeble Mindness & Autism, In The Name Of My Lord JESUS Christ, The Saviour & Healer & Deliverer & Miracle Worker!

I Speak Healing Of Injuries, Broken Bones & Fractures, In The Name Of My Lord JESUS Christ, The Saviour & Healer & Miracle Worker!

I Cast Out Every Spirit Of Sodomy/
Homosexuality, In The Name Of My Lord
JESUS Christ, The Saviour & Deliverer &
Miracle Worker!

I Break The Power & Deceit Of Witchcraft Off
You, In The Name Of My Lord JESUS Christ,
The Saviour & Deliverer & Miracle Worker!

I Rebuke Hunger & Starvation From You,
In The Name Of My Lord JESUS Christ, The
Saviour & Provider & Miracle Worker!

I Rebuke Drought & Speak Rain, In The Name
Of My Lord JESUS Christ, The Saviour &
Provider & Miracle Worker!

I Speak & Decree Heat To You When Cold &
Cool To You When Hot, In The Name Of My
Lord JESUS Christ, The Saviour & Comforter &
Miracle Worker!

I Curse & Cast Out Every Spirit Of Infirmity,
In The Name Of My Lord JESUS Christ, The
Saviour & Healer & Deliverer & Miracle
Worker!

For Those Of You Who Do Not Have The Holy
Ghost, Who Have Received The Words In This
Book, Repent As We Have Told You, Then I
Say Unto You, Receive The Holy Ghost, Speak

In Tongues, In The Name Of My Lord JESUS Christ, The Saviour & Deliverer & Comforter & Miracle Worker! If You Have Not Repented, Repent As I Have Told You & Again Read Or Hear The Immediate Above Words, You WILL Then Be Filled With The Holy Ghost, Evidenced By Speaking In Tongues As God Speaks Another Language Through You.

Remember What We Told You In This Book, If You Want To Keep The Holy Ghost, You Must Get Baptized In The Name Of JESUS Christ For The Remission Of Your Sins.

I WARN YOU! I Have Blessed You With These Things: Healings, Deliverances, Provisions & Even Through Me Some Of You Received The Holy Ghost. However, God Will Withdraw These Blessings From You, If You Get Into Disobedience Of His Word. Your Last State Will Then Be Worse Than Your First. SO SAYS THE GOD ALMIGHTY!